You're Lying!

You're Lying!

Secrets From an Expert Military
Interrogator to Spot the Lies
and Get to the Truth

By Lena Sisco

THE CAREER PRESS, INC.

Pompton Plains, NJ

YOU'RE LYING!

EDITED BY KIRSTEN DALLEY
TYPESET BY DIANA GHAZZAWI
Cover design by Matt Dorfman
Printed in the U.S.A.

To order this title, please call toll-free 1-800-CAREER-1 (NJ and Canada: 201-848-0310) to order using VISA or MasterCard, or for further information on books from Career Press.

CAREER
PRESS

The Career Press, Inc.
220 West Parkway, Unit 12
Pompton Plains, NJ 07444
www.careerpress.com

Library of Congress Cataloging-in-Publication Data

Sisco, Lena.
  You're lying : secrets from an expert military interrogator to spot the lies and get to the truth / Lena Sisco.
      pages cm
  Summary: "Lena wrote You're Lying! because no matter what your profession or life circumstances, you need the skills to take control of a situation, detect deception, and reveal the truth. While you probably won't ever have to interrogate a detainee who doesn't want to tell you about an upcoming terrorist attack--as Lena has--You're Lying! will help you deal with that salesperson trying to rip you off, the kid bullying your child who claims innocence, a cheating spouse, or dissembling boss. As the adage says, knowledge is power. Lena interrogated numerous members of Al Qaeda and the Taliban while stationed at Guantanamo Bay, Cuba, then taught those skills to Defense Department personnel for years afterward. Her ability to build rapport, accurately read body language, and employ effective questioning techniques led to numerous successes that saved American lives. You will also learn her easy-to-follow five-step program on how to accurately detect verbal (both spoken and written) and non-verbal deceptive tells, how to conduct an effective line of questioning, and what to do after you identify the lies we all face every day. Take the knowledge in You're Lying! and empower yourself. Don't get fooled again"-- Provided by publisher.
  Includes bibliographical references and index.
  ISBN 978-1-60163-362-0 (paperback) -- ISBN 978-1-60163-390-3 (ebook) 1. Deception. 2. Truthfulness and falsehood. 3. Body language. 4. Inter-personal communication. I. Title.
  BF637.D42S57 2015
  153.6--dc23
                        2015002798

To my amazing and wonderful parents, Bill and Roseann,
who have always supported me through
the many adventures in my life. I love you.

Acknowledgments

This is my first publication—hopefully the first of many—so I would like to acknowledge and thank all those who made it possible. You have no idea how much your effort, mentorship, friendship, and support mean to me.

First, I want to express my deepest gratitude to my parents, Bill and Roseann, who have been by my side as I transitioned from almost failing out of college to graduating from Brown, from studying archaeology to joining the military, from chasing the California dream to battling the Beltway, and, finally, to settling (for now) in Virginia Beach. I may not have always chosen the most successful path, but I always knew that the path would lead me to success, and so did you. I could never say thank you enough for everything you have done for me. You are the best!

I want to thank my biggest fan for always believing in me, and who never once let me stay down in the tough times. You are my pillar, and I hope one day I can be yours when you need it. Nancy Drew?

I want to thank my brother Chris for putting up with my countless demands! And especially for building my Website(s). I owe you, big time.

I want to acknowledge the rest of my awesome, fun, immediate family: Jimmy, Jill, and Katie. Christine, you'll never need a power pose to build confidence, because you were born with it. Katie and Jill, let's dance!

A very special thank you to Janine Driver, the lady who made me see it was all possible. Janine had a profound effect on me and it's because of her and the Body Language Institute that I am where I am today. She always believed in me, sometimes more than I did myself. Thanks for the push; I will always and forever be grateful for your mentorship. Thank you to Kerry Strollo, Janine's sister; you are a "fire and forget" person, and I appreciate that.

Thank you, Bulldog O'Clair, for being my gorgeous model. But even more, thanks for being real. Your support and energy helped fuel me. Hugs and kisses! And thank you, Gina and Chris, for modeling your beautiful faces. Now, where's the wine?

Thank you to Nic Smith and the Henley-Putman graduate student for sharing your stories so that I could share them with my readers. You rock!

Thank you, Maryann Karinch. Without you, I wouldn't be writing any of these thank yous! I love your sincerity and your energy. You let me scratch off an item on my bucket list.

Thank you, Career Press, for picking up my first publication. I am thrilled beyond words that this happened. I look forward to working with you on my next book, which is already in the works.

I want to thank two dear friends who always provided me with words of encouragement and wisdom, Alissa and Kristy. We partied like rock stars; I love you both to the moon and stars!

I want to raise a glass to Diane, *to us and making it happen.* Cheers!

Thank you to those I served with, especially to my GTMO family back in the day. I'm thankful that I can still keep in touch with some of you. I hope your lives have led you to success. I also want to thank every military member for your honor, courage, and commitment. It may sound clichéd, but there are really no better words to describe what you signed up for and what you do. Thank you, Dave, for the "QC."

Thank you to all of my family and friends who have inspired me to write in some way that you may not even know of; *you may just read about it in this book.*

Many thanks to all of you who are reading this, to those of you who have heard me speak, and to those of you I've trained. It's because of you that I can keep sharing my knowledge.

And lastly, I am thankful for my family of furry friends who give me so much joy and who keep me calm and sane.

Contents

Preface

I'm sure that someone at some point has said to you, "I see what you're saying," and that told you that this person understood what you just said. Wouldn't it have made more sense for him or her to have said, "I understand what you're saying"? After all, we hear people speak, but we can't *see* their speech (unless they are speaking in sign language, of course). So how, then, can we see what people say? We can't. But we can see *how* people say things—their body language, their facial expressions, the things they do while they speak—and that makes us feel that we can actually see what they say, beyond just their spoken words. For example, I can observe how people lie through words, body gestures, facial expressions, and certain physiological signs.

When I hear people say "I see what you're saying," it tells me that they "get" me. It reminds me of greeting of the Na'vi people, the indigenous, albeit fictitious, culture on the planet Pandora in James Cameron's movie *Avatar*. Their greeting is "I see you," which essentially translates as "I can see into your soul and I know you. *I get you.*" This book is intended to expound on the relationships among hearing, listening, and seeing: hearing the sounds people make, listening to the specific words they use, and seeing their body gestures and facial expressions while they speak.

When what we say and how we say it (through body language) match up, it's called *behavioral congruency*. When they don't match, we have *behavioral incongruency*; in this case, the body isn't matching up with the words being said or the true emotions behind those words. I will teach you how to spot both of these. I will also teach you how to look for deceptive *tells* (deviations from normal behavior that indicate stress) and why you have to look for clusters of these tells to determine whether someone is lying. Understanding what people say goes far beyond just hearing their words, although words and the voice play a key part in detecting deception, as you will soon find out. In fact, I tend to rely more on verbal deceptive tells than nonverbal. I will explain why later on, as you begin to understand the complexities of nonverbal communication.

In *Avatar*, when the Na'vi say "I see you," they are saying they can sense the true emotions and inner spirit of others; they can empathize. Empathy is key to building rapport, and building rapport is the process of earning likeability, trust, and respect. Because I practice yoga, I see a connection between the Na'vi greeting and the *Sanskrit* word *namaste*. After the end of each yoga session, I say *namaste*. This word encapsulates my belief that there is a divine spark within each of us that is located in the heart chakra; it is an acknowledgment of the soul in one by the soul in another. You've probably heard the idea that if you look deeply into someone's eyes, you can see into his or her soul. Have you ever wondered what is so special about the soul? The soul is the true essence of the self; there is no hiding it, deceiving others about it, or faking it. So we know when we aren't being honest with ourselves, and we know when we are lying to others; we can't fool ourselves! And why do you suppose the eyes are the gateway to the soul? Perhaps it's because the eyes are so expressive, and the fact that it's almost impossible to control their movements and thus hide one's true feelings or emotions. If you want to be a body-language expert and use body language to help you detect deception, build rapport, and enhance your overall interpersonal communication skills, you'll need to be able to determine the true emotions behind what people say, in addition to the meaning of the words they choose. Done correctly, this is when the art and science of human interaction meet. You won't be able to see someone's soul after reading this book, but you will be able to know when people aren't being honest with themselves and, more importantly, you. And that's the whole reason I wrote this book in the first place.

Namaste.

Introduction

"You are so nice; you should become Muslim. But you have to realize that even though I like you, if I see you on the streets, I'll have to kill you." This is what a detainee once told me while I was interrogating him at Guantanamo Bay, Cuba, otherwise referred to as Gitmo, or GTMO, which stands for Guantanamo. I was happy that I was able to build rapport with him and obtain information from him; I just had to make sure to never run into him on the streets. (I'm not worried I ever will.)

I wrote this book to share my experiences and my knowledge of interpersonal communication, rapport-building, body language, and detecting deception. In this book you will learn the myths surrounding deception-detecting techniques, and why body language is thought of as a voodoo science among many professionals, and hence why it so frequently discredited. You will also learn how and why it works through my easy-to-follow, five-step body language program, "Be a Body Language Expert: Be a REBLE." This program teaches you how to accurately read body language, detect verbal and nonverbal deception, and get to the truth. After all, what's the point of being able to read body language and detect deception if you can't ultimately get the truth out of someone?

You will get a glimpse into the life of a female interrogator through my personal stories as I share my secrets about how I built rapport with terrorists, gained their trust, and found out what they knew. I will also teach you my rule of three when it comes to baselining people (a necessity before you even begin to think you can detect deception), how to accurately detect verbal (spoken and written) and nonverbal deceptive tells, and then what to do with this information once you have it. I will teach you how to use good questioning techniques, how to control a conversation, and how to extract the truth while maintaining rapport.

Wittingly or unwittingly, people use body language every day to communicate with others, to interact with others, and to build up (or tear down) their relationships with others. (I've always thought the study of body language should be included in the social sciences, because social science by definition is the study of relationships among individuals in a society.) You will learn how to build amazing relationships with people, inspire yourself and others, earn people's trust, and make them want to be truthful and honest with you. This book will not only teach you how to accurately read body language to detect deception, but it will also offer you a plethora of tools to build self-confidence and enhance your interpersonal communication skills. I used these tools as a military interrogator to extract information from members of al Qaeda and the Taliban in order to save lives and convict terrorists of war crimes. Law enforcement personnel and investigators will benefit from the techniques I teach in this book, but anyone—salespeople, doctors and nurses, lawyers and judges, teachers, counselors and therapists, just to name a few—can use these tools in their everyday life. You'll be able to get the raise or promotion you deserve, detect if your children are lying to you about using drugs, put your clients at ease by establishing rapport and understanding what they really want, determine whether your witness is withholding information, adjust your body language to better communicate with people, and exude confidence and get people to want to trust, respect, and follow you. You will also be better able to connect with your colleagues to finish team assignments, increase your profit margin by boosting your clientele, gain a criminal's trust and respect in order to elicit a confession, and understand and heed your "gut feeling" when you feel that someone isn't telling you the *whole* truth and get to the truth without losing rapport.

After reading and digesting the information in the following pages, you will have the confidence to decode body language by recognizing verbal and nonverbal deceptive tells, and thereby identify when someone is getting one over on you in both your personal and your professional life. Many of us will get a gut feeling when we are being taken advantage of, but oftentimes we either don't trust that feeling or know what to do when we have it. My program will allow you to *trust your gut*, because you will understand why you have that feeling in the first place, and enable you to stand up for yourself by getting what you deserve: respect and the truth. Will it help you figure out whether your significant other is lying to you, or whether your spouse is cheating on you? Will it help you beat a hand a poker? Will it help you get a date with the object of your affection? Will it help you win the next big contract? The answer to all of those questions and more is a resounding yes.

Countless books have been published about reading body language, detecting deception, and building rapport, some of which were written by distinguished colleagues of mine and which I own. This book is a unique take on these endeavors from my personal point of view, enriched with my unique experiences and lessons learned that I'd like to pass on to you. I designed this book to be both educational and entertaining. The final chapter includes a checklist/quick reference guide to of all the new tools and techniques you will have learned. My challenge to you is to learn what I am about to teach you and then use it!

I teach body language for three reasons: first, I am passionate about it; second, it works whether you are trying to build rapport, enhance your communications skills, spot the lies, or get the truth; and third, everybody who interacts with other human beings, no matter what their profession, should have these skills. My goal is to mentor people on all of these skills so they can succeed in life and not be taken advantage of or be deceived by others.

I learned body language primarily by doing it, not by reading about it. I never took a psychology class, nor was I trained in the workings of the human mind by a professional. My experience in body language and interpersonal communication comes from my former life as an archaeologist, from my degrees in anthropology/archaeology, from a one-hour class (called "Enemy Prisoner of War") I was required to take during my interrogation training, and then from the literally hundreds of hours I spent interrogating members of al Qaeda and the Taliban during the global war on terror. After learning essentially by trial and error, I then dove into conducting self-study research on body language and human emotions and interactions, and attended specialized training by other experts. I taught myself personality profiling from Jungian type personality preferences and handwriting analysis, which I then used to mentor my own students for two years to see whether they helped me communicate with them (hint: They did).

I truly hope my experiences and the knowledge I share with you in this book will bring you personal and professional success. Enjoy learning about the interaction between the art and the science of human behavior, and use my program to empower your life, one day at a time.

1

You Are Not a Mind Reader: Uncover the Primary Myth About Detecting Deception

Did you know that the only universal language is body language? It is virtually the same across all cultures, genders, and ages. The only aspects of body language affected culturally are specific head and hand gestures and the concept of personal space. Signs of anxiety and stress, and displays of emotions are the same. Despite this, detecting deception is an inexact science. It is also difficult. I am not trying to discourage you; I just want to prepare you for this reality. You will need to rely on a toolbox of advanced techniques as well as your ability to identify hundreds of nonverbal and verbal *tells* (changes or deviations from a person's normal behavior), and then determine whether someone is lying or not. If you figure out that someone is lying, you then have the responsibility, to yourself and others, to get to the truth. Detecting deception is only half of the task; extracting the truth is the other half. If you are not going to work to get the truth, why bother trying to detect deception at all? What good would it do you?

It's easy to learn about common deceptive, nonverbal *tells* (deviations from the norm such as crossing the arms, rapid blinking, shoulder shrugging, and trying to disguise a smile) in someone's body language, but these tells in and of themselves are not necessarily indicative of deception. Some of them merely indicate contemplation, stress, anxiety, or even embarrassment. As a former DoD certified military interrogator, I detected deception, both verbal and nonverbal, in my detainees pretty often. I was pretty accurate, but not 100 percent of the time. I challenge anyone who considers him- or herself an expert in detecting deception and who states that he or she is always right. Some people use the term "deception-detecting expert" to describe themselves; others use "body-language expert." I prefer the latter because I don't believe anyone can accurately detect deception all the time. That said, we can come pretty darn close, maybe even 99 percent of the time. I have used all the tools and techniques I teach in this book, and have had great success with them based on the actionable intelligence I collected that resulted in the identification of terrorists and foreign fighters, their missions, the locations of their training camps, how they were trained, how they were financed, how they recruited new members, how they communicated and traveled, and how they viewed the West. This information helped us thwart future attacks, capture other terrorists, and save lives.

When I tell people I read body language, I can't tell you how many times they respond by asking me, "So, what am I thinking right now?" I can read the body but I can't read the mind, although I wish I could! Even my company motto differentiates the two: "Move the body to influence the mind; read the body to influence people." Meaning, when I teach people how to feel confident so they can speak in pub- lic or ace a job interview, I tell them they have to first look confident. Once they move their body and assume, say, a confidence or power pose, which I'll talk about in Chapter 5, they will start to *feel* confi- dent. I used to tell my students, "If you feel stupid, you look stupid." Fortunately the converse is also true: If you look confident, you will feel confident. When you learn to accurately read body language— and you will be able to do just that after reading this book—you will be able to influence people to like, respect, trust, and be honest with you. So to make it clear, I can't read minds, but I can read your facial expressions and body gestures, which can tell me an awful lot about what's really going through your mind when you tell me, "I swear it wasn't me!" as you turn sideways, shrug your shoulders, and try to hide a smile. I will know that what you are really saying is "It *was* me." But I still can't read your mind!

Today countless individuals, companies, and institutions teach the private sector how to read nonverbal communication to enhance communication skills, confidence, and rapport. These skills have rewarded everyone from small-business owners to huge corporations. For every one person who teaches it, however, there seem to be 20 who refute it and refer to it as a voodoo science—hokey at best, and unreliable at worst. The problem lies with how reading body language and detecting deception are taught and learned. For example, many people think that just because they watch the *Lie to Me* series on TV, they are body-language experts, but the show neglects two very important elements of identifying deception and finding the truth: establishing a person's baseline behavior (so that you can identify behavioral incongruence—more on that later), and knowing how to identify the exact moment you see that incongruence and then probe with precise questions to understand why there was a shift in behavior in the first place. Was he lying, or was it something else? The old method of interpreting body language to detect deception led people to believe that the observation of one particular body gesture was indicative of deception and automatically meant that person was lying. Just because someone shrugs her shoulders when she says, "I don't know what happened to the money you left on the counter," doesn't mean she knows where the money is and she is lying to you. A shoulder shrug always indicates uncertainty, but in this case it doesn't necessarily mean that this person is uncertain about the whereabouts of the money; it could mean she was thinking of the check she just bounced and was wondering where all *her* money went. Something to keep in mind is that when you falsely accuse someone of lying, you may lose both that person's trust and your credibility.

Some people who take body-language training think they have become mind readers. This couldn't be further from the truth. If you have ever watched the magician Criss Angel, you would swear he was a mind reader. Guess what? He's not. He creates illusions, he influences people, and he reads body language (including facial micro-expressions), and he is great at all of it. He once had Oprah think of a number from 1 to 100 so that he could try to guess it, and of course he did. The number was 11. Here's how he did it. First, he planted his foregone success in Oprah's mind by saying, "I'm [going to] show you how I use psychology and how I study your mannerisms to get inside your head, Oprah, and tell you what you're thinking." As he began to "chunk" groups of numbers to narrow down which one contained the number Oprah was thinking about, her eyes widened ever so slightly and her mouth opened when he asked her, "Is your number between 1 and 15?" Her eyes and the expression on her face told him everything he needed to know. Now, I am sure Criss uses other magician's techniques that I am not privy to, but even so, his guess was confirmed by her facial micro-expression.

But how did he come up with 11? Have you ever wondered why you always seem to look at a clock when it's 11:11? I do this almost daily. Numerologists believe that 11:11 represents synchronicity, meaning that taking note of the number is not a casual coincidence but instead a purposeful coincidence. Carl Jung, the Swiss psychologist whom I will talk more about in Chapter 7, was the first to write about synchronicity. He described in very scientific prose how events that seem to be coincidental at first, often aren't, but are in fact causally related. I like to sum up his theory with my favorite phrase: Everything happens for a reason. But back to the number 11. Why do we look at the clock when it is 11:11, why did Oprah pick the number 11, and why are there 11 chapters in this book? All coincidence? Or are we all subconsciously drawn to see, write, and think about 11? Unfortunately I do not have answers to these questions, but the fact that Oprah chose a synchronous number to begin with, and that fact that Criss saw her mouth open slightly and her eyes widen ever so subtly in surprise as he honed in on her number, could have assisted him in guessing correctly. Also, when Oprah initially wrote down the number on a large pad of white paper to show the audience, she used upstrokes on the 1s, the European way of writing the number 1, not just plain, vertical lines, the American way. Apparently someone in the audience asked what the number was, perhaps because she had never seen 1s written that way, so Criss was able to hear Oprah ask her audience, "For goodness' sake, you don't know what that is?" The audience laughed, and she rewrote 11, this time using the Palmer method of handwriting, with just vertical lines, and showed her audience again. They laughed more loudly, and she asked, "Okay, everybody got it okay?" Criss must have known there are only two numbers that can be written differently, one and seven. As a former archaeologist I was taught to write numbers as they do in continental Europe to avoid confusion, so I put hooks on my ones and slashes through my sevens. The bottom line is—and I bet he would tell you this, too—Criss Angel is not a mind reader, but he is very observant and sees a lot of things that most people don't. After reading this book, you, too, will learn to see some of those things that Criss Angel, I, and other body-language experts can see, and then use them to your advantage. When you learn how to accurately read body language and detect deceptive tells, you will for all intents and purposes become an analyst.

There is an entire process to knowing how to use body language to detect deception. This process should always follow what I call the rule of three, which I will talk about in Chapter 8. In brief, you need to study a person's body language to establish his normal body language behavior (the *baseline*), and then match up what is being said verbally to what is being said nonverbally through specific body gestures, looking for deviations from the baseline (*tells*). But one tell is not enough: You need to look for clusters of tells and then evaluate the context in which you see them. After you get a feel for someone's baseline body language, you will be able to pick up on when it changes. For example, I am from Rhode Island and I'm half Italian, so when I talk, I talk loudly and quickly, with my arms swinging away. In fact, when I'm really excited, I've been known to accidentally hit people while I'm talking. This is normal body language behavior for me. If at any point I were to quiet my arm and hand movements while I was speaking, this would indicate a deviation from my baseline behavior. Was it because I lied? At this point you'd have no idea, but you'd know it's a deviation, a *tell*, and that tells you to probe further. Again, one tell alone will not indicate deception; clusters of tells will. If you were trying to find out whether I was lying, you would need to probe the subject I was speaking about right when you saw the deviation, by using carefully formulated questions to see whether you could observe another tell. As you can see, the process of detecting deception is not as simple as people think. It's a methodical process, and I will teach you this process in the following chapters.

You will also learn how and why people lie and deceive, along with techniques for how to extract to the truth from someone while maintaining respect and rapport. Wouldn't you want to know how to get hardened criminals to like you *and* want to tell you the truth? Wouldn't you want to know how to get the upper hand in a competitive situation, how to make a killer first impression, how to feel and look more confident, how to get people to want to listen to what you have to say, and how to get people to look at you as a leader and respect you? Wouldn't you want to know if your new employee was stealing money from your business? Whether your daughter was being bullied? Whether your son was using drugs? Whether your coworker lied to your boss to get the promotion you were both up for? Whether your witness was purposefully omitting details in his testimony? Whether a convicted felon lied about the whereabouts of his victims? Whether a job candidate lied about her qualifications? Whether your patient lied to you to get prescription drugs? If you answered yes to *any* of these questions and want to take the skills I am about to teach you to attain success in your professional and personal life, then read on.

It is my belief that everyone, no matter what their professional or personal goals, should have these skills to take control of their lives, detect deception, garner respect, and know the truth. Whether you're talking about a detainee who doesn't want to tell you about an upcoming terror attack, a salesperson who is trying to rip you off, or a kid who is bullying your child but claims innocence, *knowledge is powerful*. Take the knowledge I am giving you here and use it in your everyday life. This book isn't just about an interrogator sharing her tricks of trade to catch liars; it's about improving how you interact with people overall.

Of course, catching liars is my forté. When I was being trained as an interrogator, I was taught all kinds of interrogation techniques, from building rapport, detecting deception, EPW (enemy prisoner of war) psychology, cross-cultural communications, how to properly ask questions and fully exploit information, how to work with interpreters, and, finally, how to report the information I collected. The three techniques that gave me the most consistent success, however, were building rapport, identifying verbal and nonverbal deceptive tells, and using advanced questioning techniques. If you decide to make a career out of reading body language and detecting deception, whether it is in teaching people these skills as a motivational speaker or using them in a profession, as I did, your credibility (and perhaps the credibility and life of the individual you are reading) is always on the line. Forewarned is forearmed!

2

Why Do People Lie?

We all lie. Yes, even you! People lie for numerous reasons. Some people lie for self-preservation, protecting themselves from fear, pain, guilt, shame, and/or embarrassment. Some people lie to protect others' feelings. People lie to fit in, to evade conflict, or to avoid hurting someone they love. Some people lie because it's their job; others lie just because they like to feel they are getting away with something or getting one over on someone else. Then there are the charming sociopaths who lie incessantly to get their way with no concern for others; the compulsive liars who lie out of habit and feel awkward when telling the truth; the professional liars, who master the art of lie to get the job done, and then there is everybody else; and the list goes on and on. Because we all lie.

You may be thinking, *Who is she to tell me I lie*? Think about when your phone rings at home and you know it's someone you really don't want to talk to. Have you ever told someone (your spouse or your child) to tell that person you are not available or not at home? Well, guess what? You just lied. Or think about when your best friend came to you and asked, "What do you think of my new skinny jeans?" when said jeans were noticeably two sizes too skinny, and you said, "They look great!" while thinking, *How on earth did she get in them?* Or the time your mom called and asked, "Did you remember that Dad's birthday is Friday?" and you say, "Of course I did, Mom!" as you wrote, "Get Dad birthday card" on a sticky note. What about when the doctor asks you how often you exercise and you say, "Three times a week," knowing darn well that you squeeze in a 20-minute walk once a week if you're lucky? I don't even have to say it, because you know you're lying.

When I was in the military I was considered to be a professional liar. I told detainees responsible for acts of terrorisms that I would do everything in my power to get them out of prison and released back to their country of origin; I told Taliban members I understood why they fought jihad against Westerners and that the United States should have never entered Afghanistan; I even sympathized and empathized with hardcore terrorists about their capture and imprisonment. I lied because it was my job to do so, in order to get information.

Three Ways to Lie

There are three ways to lie: the false statement, embellishment, and lying by omission. You can lie by saying something that is completely untrue, you can embellish the details of a story, or you can leave out a detail or details of a story. Did you know that nine out of 10 people lie on their resumes by embellishing their skills and responsibilities? Wouldn't you want to know that if you were a hiring manager? I work with a bunch of type-A personalities; heck, I'm one myself. We are very competitive and have to be the best at everything. When our war stories start circulating, the details seem to get more and more exciting and badass each time. Could there be some slight embellishment going on here? Most likely, but the stories are always entertaining!

An example of lying by omission would be when your wife asks you, "Who's going on the business trip with you tomorrow?" and you know that the young, attractive, single paralegal the firm just hired is going, but you only say, "John and Pete"—that is lying by omission. You're not saying she isn't going, but you're not telling your wife she is, either. Perhaps your sole reason for lying by omission is that you don't want to cause any concern for your wife, because you have absolutely no interest in the 20-year-old paralegal and are happily married. If that's the case, then why lie by omitting the fact she's going? For many of the reasons I have already listed previously. Lying is not always done for personal gratification; it may be done to spare the feelings of others or just to keep the peace.

In relationships the key thing is to know the preferred communication style of the other person. Does he prefer you keep the peace and omit unnecessary facts? Or does he prefer you to be open and forthright about every detail, no matter what the consequence? Whichever way it is, you have to respect and exercise his preferred style, even if it's not your preference, or at least meet him halfway. Relationships are about trust and communication. You can't have one without the other, and without both, you have no relationship. My most successful relationships, friendships and intimate, have been when both parties are equally open and honest. Once you know the worst about your friend or spouse, then there's only the best to come. We are all human and we all make mistakes and misjudgments. Let's face it: We all have screwed up at least once. I've told people some of my worst mistakes, but if they still like and respect me after that, I know I have a solid relationship. So, when it comes to deciding whether you should tell your friend that her jeans are too tight, or tell your wife that the young blond is going on the business trip with you, think about her, not you, and what she would prefer to hear. It may be that your friend says, "Yeah, I guess these can be my goal pants for when I drop 10 more pounds. Thanks for being so honest!" Or maybe your wife says, "I don't really care; just miss me and come back ready to spend some alone time, with no kids!" I will say for the record that 30 minutes of an uncomfortable conversation beats a lifetime of regret or subterfuge. When you learn to accept your mistakes and foibles, you will begin to more easily accept those of others, and that in turn will create a mutual respect—all from allowing yourselves to be human with each other. My advice? Don't be afraid to share everything, but first make sure you know whether the person wants to hear it or not!

Two Types of Liars

The imploders

So now that we understand everyone lies or has lied at some point, I am going to tell you about the two types of liars: those who implode—everyday liars, and those who explode—powerful liars. Imploders, or everyday liars feel nervous about lying, so their stress increases when they lie. The stress hormone *cortisol* is released, and the body goes through some physiological responses to the stress such as dry mouth, flushing, and sweating, just to name a few. The stress caused by lying heightens their senses and they become paranoid. They feel as though everyone can see their lie, so they try to vanish by physically making themselves smaller (imploding) by slouching, turning their shoulders inward, avoiding eye contact, crossing their legs and arms—essentially balling up. Their voice will weaken but become higher pitched. They will use distancing language to remove themselves from the lie. (I'll discuss more about what happens to the body when it's under stress in Chapter 5.)

At this point their cognitive thinking starts to deteriorate, and they won't be able to remember the details of the lie they just told. In Chapter 10 I will teach you techniques on how to catch someone in a lie; many of these techniques exploit the fact that cognition decreases while imploders are lying. J.J. Newberry, retired Senior Special Agent with the Bureau of Alcohol, Tobacco and Firearms (and part of a select group of individuals known as Truth Wizards, who have been tested and rated by Dr. Paul Ekman and Dr. Maureen O'Sullivan as the best of the best at detecting deception) describes studies that have shown how cognitive thinking, which involves the brain's critical skills of attention, long- and short-term memory, processing speed, visual and auditory processing, and logic and reasoning, actually *lowers* behavioral animation (see: *www.psychologytoday .com/experts/mr-jj-newberry* and *www.forensicpsychologyunbound .ws/OAJFP/Volume_2__2010_files/Vrij,%20et%20al.%202010.pdf*). This means that, as liars are in the midst of spinning a lie, their body languagequiets down while their brain is processing at full capacity, but immediately before and after the lie, they leak deceptive *tells* (departures from their normal behavior that indicate stress).

Everyday liars like you and me will tend to get nervous and anxious as we lie, and our bodies will reveal that anxiety and stress through visible physiological responses. We will mess up details of a story or forget them completely, we will unknowingly change verb tenses and pronouns, and we will exhibit clusters of nonverbal deceptive tells, which you will learn about in the following pages.

The exploders

Powerful liars, the exploders, will do just the opposite of everyday liars. They actually physically expand by making themselves appear bigger, so that they will look and feel more confident and in control. They may take up more room with arm gestures, by widening their stance, and by becoming louder and more animated. They use the "convince, not convey" technique: Truthful people *convey* a story, whereas liars try to *convince* you of a story. Powerful liars often enjoy lying. Instead of cortisol, the stress hormone *dopamine* is released. Dopamine is a complex chemical in the body that passes information from one neuron to the next via the *mesolimbic pathway*, which is associated with addictions and sexual arousal. Dopamine is too complex for scientists to define so I am not going to try to do it here. What is important to know is that powerful liars don't get nervous when they lie; they get off on it; it gives them a high. Hence their cognitive thinking doesn't decrease; it increases. Some powerful liars even have a kind of a God complex: They think they are better than everyone else and so good at lying that they'll never be caught by a *normal* person. They think you would have to be as clever and smart as they are in order for you to catch them. But guess what? Powerful liars still exhibit deceptive tells, and this is where you can catch them!

People often ask me, a former interrogator and "professional" liar, how I broke detainees' will to resist telling the truth and their determination to keep telling lies. My response is because I attract more bees with honey than vinegar. I am a 5-feet, 4-inch-tall female, I weigh 125 pounds, and I am most certainly not intimidating. Instead of trying to get the detainees to fear me, I got them to like me; some even came to respect what I was doing. In fact, I was invited to Pakistan to dinner to meet one detainee's family; another sketched a picture of me and transcribed on the back, "Good luck for success in your work." My *work*, you realize, was interrogating him. I'm a good salesperson. I sold them the idea of freedom in exchange for information, freedom I knew most wouldn't get and most certainly didn't deserve, but I was still able to convince them freedom was attainable if they cooperated and told the truth. (Remember: I'm lying to them about freedom so I have to convince them, not convey to them.) Obviously there is a lot more to how I actually got to the truth, which I'll explain to you in bits and pieces throughout this book.

Despite the recent release of the Committee Study of the Central Intelligence Agency's Detention and Interrogation Program, compiled by the Senate Select Committee on Intelligence, I stand by my words when I say that during my time spent at GTMO as a DoD certified military interrogator from August to December 2002, I never heard of, knew of, or saw any detainee physically or mentally abused, coerced, or "tortured." Based on the news, unfortunately, it seems that it may have happened at other sites. But just to be clear, I did not, nor did any member of the DoD that I worked with in GTMO during the time I was there, torture detainees. To the contrary, our detainees got tea, trail mix, movies, books, games, candy, and any other incentive item they requested to make their life in prison more tolerable. In fact, we even took extra steps to import delicacies from their countries of origin. Based on our discoveries that respect and rapport got us information, years after I left, special camps were built for cooperative detainees where they could play soccer and grow their own gardens. This to me seems to be a far cry from torture.

I took the stand a few years ago and swore to the same thing I have written here, but apparently there are people in the world who claim for a fact this happened without ever having set foot on the island.

Unfortunately, I was a victim of press articles stating I said things I didn't and did things I had no knowledge of. My favorite is when my mother called me, very upset, and said, "I read that article about you by some columnist in D.C. saying you were a 'MILF'! I didn't even know what that was; your brothers had to tell me!" So thank you, un-informed columnist in D.C., who shall remain nameless, for making yourself look stupid by writing about something about which you had not a clue. Because you just proved a statistic.

How did I sell freedom? I had to lie. How did I convince detainees of my lies? Simply put, I know how to lie. But even so, I wasn't com-fortable doing it because I still feared they would see right through me.

In general, though, you feel good and you respect yourself when you are truthful, and therefore others will respect you, too. If you tend to lie, you will not respect yourself or others, and in fact you will become very distrusting of others. Did you know that people who generally distrust others do not make good detectors of deception? This is because they think everything is a lie and that every action is done for a selfish purpose. They see deception everywhere, even in truthful individuals. So if you are one of those people who don't trust anyone, you are going to have a very difficult time detecting true deception.

If you were to ask me whether there are any good reasons to lie, my answer is no. The older I get, the less I care about hurting some-one's feelings by being fake; in fact, I think being fake to someone is worse than possibly hurting their feelings and telling them the truth. I'd much rather give them the truth so they can see themselves through another set of eyes or perspective. Being (sometimes bru-tally) honest with people takes getting used to, but I have found I am more respected and have stronger relationships for doing so. I wish I had always been like this, but I lacked the confidence to be truthful when I was younger. That said, I will still lie for a job that requires me to do so for a greater good.

Knowing I prefer to speak the truth, you will learn how and why those people who do *not* like to speak the truth are good at telling a lie. I am not advocating that you practice becoming a good liar by embracing the following steps; but even if you do, you'll most likely still leak deceptive tells anyway, because most of you reading this are not professional, sociopathic, or compulsive liars. However, knowing how people get good at lying will help you detect their lies.

The Four Secrets to Being a Good Liar

1. Remain confident.

First, convince yourself of the lie, or convince yourself that you are not lying. This takes a lot of mind-over-matter power. You have to consciously trick your subconscious into thinking that you are not lying. Stay calm and say to yourself, *This is the truth.* (It's better to say that instead of *This is not a lie*, because it's easier to feel positive about a positive statement than a negative statement.) Second, make sure that part of your lie is actually true. This way you can concentrate on the truthful part to calm yourself. Once you convince yourself that what you are about to say is the truth, you will suppress the release of cortisol that would otherwise make your body respond physiologically to nervousness with an increased pulse rate, sweating, dry mouth, flushing, shaking, voice quivering, and so on. People who lie by omission and embellishment can lie more easily because there is some truth to the story. Telling a flat-out lie is harder. For this reason, many liars try to control the conversation and only talk about the parts that are true. Most people inherently want to be honest. No one likes to lie—unless you are a sociopath; even terrorists don't like it. They would rather shout to the rooftops, "We're attacking your compound tonight, you dirty American!"

2. The devil is in the details.

This is a common saying among interrogators. I used to say it to my students all the time to stress the importance of getting detailed information. The reason for this was twofold. First, if details are present in a story it gives the interrogator leverage to catch a lie because remembering details is difficult, especially when those details are made up; and second, the absence of details is a sure sign that those details are either unknown or being covered up. If an interrogator overlooks the details, he or she will never catch the lie or be able to extract the truth from a detainee. You can unravel a lie by questioning the details in the lie because, typically, liars cannot remember the details of a lie when questioned on them later.

In order to avoid this uncomfortable circumstance, good liars avoid giving details. Instead, they offer confusing and vague information that needs further questioning to explain. This in turn often makes the questioner aggravated and frustrated, because he or she knows he or she isn't getting any pertinent information. If the questioner becomes frustrated, the person telling the lie actually starts to gain the upper hand by remaining calm and taking control of the conversation (often by saying something patronizing such as "I notice you are becoming upset or angry; I'm *telling* you everything I remember"). Liars create a lie in the present tense because it never happened. When questioned on the lie, they may slip up and start telling the story in the present tense. This is a sure verbal deceptive tell that allows interrogators to discover the lie and get to the truth. So if you're trying to be a good liar, you should avoid giving up details. Speak in generalities. I will talk in greater depth about this in Chapter 10.

3. Plan and prepare.

Anticipate questions that will be asked of you and come up with your answers. When answering questions, liars try not to be wordy but often are. Liars are easy to catch when they start talking nonsense. Janine Driver calls this "double-talk." For example, liars tend to provide alibis or character witnesses in their stories, but refuse to answer questions about them with a simple yes or no. Anthony Weiner and Bill Clinton were notorious for this. Look at this transcription of the Fox News clip of Representative Weiner defending his handling of the photo scandal:

Reporter: "This is not that situation. You said, from your Twitter account, a lewd photograph was sent to a college student. Answer the question: was it from you or not? Did you send it or not?"

Wiener: "If I were giving a speech to a 45,000 people and someone in the back threw a pie or yelled out an insult, I would not spend the next two hours of my speech responding to that pie or insult."

Reporter: "All you have to do is say no."

(To watch the video online, go to *www.youtube.com/watch?v=05-_LIOd5nM.*)

I agree. All Weiner had to do was say no, but he couldn't (or wouldn't) because then he would have lied on television. Didn't he understand that the fact he couldn't (or wouldn't) give a direct answer told everyone watching that he was lying? You would think that his public relations assistant would have coached him better. And what is this pie reference? Do people typically throw pies from the back of a room filled with 45,000 people? I don't think a pie would actually reach the stage—just a thought. The pie reference was Wiener's nonsense language, a story meant to get us focused on the pie rather than what he had done (or claimed not to have done).

Now look at this transcription of President Bill Clinton giving his testimony regarding Monica Lewinsky:

Reporter: "If Monica Lewinsky says that while you were in the Oval Office area you touched her breasts, would she be lying?"

Clinton: [*pause*] "Let me say something about all this—"

Reporter: "All I really need for you, Mr. President, is to [say] I won't answer under the previous grounds, or, or to answer the question, you see, because we only have four hours and your answers are extremely lengthy."

Clinton: "I know. But go ahead and ask your questions."

Reporter: "Question is, if Monica Lewinsky says that while you were in the Oval Office area you touched her breasts, would she be lying?"

Clinton: "That is not my recollection. My recollection is that I did not have sexual relations with Ms. Lewinsky and I am staying on my former statement about that."

(Watch the full video here: *www.youtube.comwatch?v=ClfpG2-1Bv4*.)

Bill Clinton had the same problem Anthony Wiener had; he just couldn't say no. This proves my point that people inherently do not like to lie. And they certainly do not want to lie on television, in front of a grand jury and thousands of viewers. So if you want to get away with a lie, answer yes or no to a yes-or-no question. (I will talk more about the liar's inability to answer this kind of question in Chapter 10.)

4. Be congruent in your body language.

This is probably the most difficult step to master. In fact, most people can't do it. In order to display *behavioral congruency*, which is having your body language match up to the words you are saying, you have to know your baseline behavior when you are not being deceptive. Unless someone who reads body language has told you what your body language is saying when you are not being deceptive, you probably don't know what your baseline behavior is. I will talk in depth about reading and establishing someone's baseline behavior in Chapter 8, which covers the third step in my five-step program. Your baseline will tell others what you do with your eyes, your body, your voice, your patterns of speech, and your facial expressions. It will also identify the physiological responses you are most likely to exhibit. If you are not an exploder (powerful liar), you will exhibit *behavioral incongruences*—that is, deceptive tells.

And finally, you need to know that liars will try to convince you with information and truthful people will convey information. If someone is working really hard to convince you they were home last night and not out with *friends*, or that they didn't know anything about the robbery that happened next door, and your gut feeling is saying not to trust them, you may want to trust your gut, but don't make any hasty judgments; read this book and you will learn both how and how *not* to get to the truth.

Lying is difficult. You may think you're good at it, but I guarantee you are still leaking deceptive tells that you are not even aware of. It is extremely hard to suppress cortisol when you lie because you will be nervous. Even though we all lie, most of us prefer to be honest; we also like to think that others prefer to be honest with us. We tend to like people who are attractive, who smile, and who speak in a low-pitched voice, because they seem more trustworthy and powerful. What I can say for certain is that people will still try to lie even though the odds of being caught are very high. Although we all lie, no one should be lied to.

3

The Human Lie Detector Versus the Lie Detector Machine

"I'm telling you the truth."

Wouldn't it be great if you could always believe that? Unfortunately, neither a body-language expert nor a polygraph machine can determine whether that statement is truthful with 100-percent accuracy, 100 percent of the time. Nevertheless, I have more trust in the body-language expert to detect deception than I do a polygraph machine. Did you know that the polygraph machine can't detect lies? It detects stress, so it should actually be called a stress-detector machine. Do most people show signs of stress when they lie? Absolutely! But not everyone does.

So why, then, do interrogators, police, courts of law, and intelligence agencies rely on polygraphs to find out whether people are lying? The answer most would give is that when people lie, they experience stress, and the polygraph machine picks up on that stress. These institutions assume that all people stress out and exhibit signs of anxiety when they lie. I have already discussed the two types of liars in the previous chapter, everyday liars (imploders) and powerful liars (exploders), so you already know that powerful liars don't get stressed out when they lie, because their body isn't releasing cortisol, the stress hormone. So, if I were to hook up a powerful liar to a polygraph machine, he or she would likely pass the test. It's probably also the reason why so many spies in the United States have passed the polygraph and were incorrectly exonerated from accusations of stealing and selling our nation's intelligence secrets. For example, Anna Belen Montes, a Cuban spy, was an analyst working for the Defense Intelligence Agency (DIA) and passed multiple polygraph tests during her 16 years of employment there. Aldrich Ames worked at the Central Intelligence Agency (CIA) for years and passed periodic polygraph examinations while he was selling U.S. government secrets to the Soviet Union along with the names of CIA operatives working in the Soviet Union. His treason cost the lives of 11 CIA operatives working in the Soviet Union at that time (they were killed by the KGB). According to Ames, "There is no trick to [passing the polygraph]; just smile and make the examiner think you like them" (source: *www.cvsa1.com/polygraphfailures .htm*). Larry Wu-Tai Chin, a CIA analyst, also passed periodic polygraph examinations before he was caught spying for China. These are just three examples, but there are many more.

Anyone working for the government, whether as a civilian, a contractor, or a member of the military, has to first take a polygraph test to obtain and maintain a specific type of security clearance to see whether they can be trusted safeguarding our nation's secrets. I took a polygraph and passed with flying colors in a record time—15 minutes. Before I took it, I heard horror stories from my colleagues, many of whom had to go back and take the test three or more times because their results were "inconclusive." My polygrapher worried me more than being hooked up to that crazy machine. He was a tall, lanky man, with black hair, a black, closely trimmed beard, black-rimmed glasses, and was dressed in a striped, short-sleeved shirt and blue pants. He looked like he had just stepped out of the year 1972. I'll never forget him. He was far from personable, but I did what he asked and answered his questions with a yes or no, and no more. After I completed the examination, I thought, *That's it? What's all the hype about?* He told me to go wait in the lobby. After about 10 minutes he appeared in the doorway (cracked open only enough to reveal his face) and said, "You may have to come back; your results are inconclusive." *Shocker,* I thought. I smiled widely and said, "No problem." At that point I knew he just wanted to intimidate me. I wanted to tell him, "Listen, buddy. I just got back from working in a prison where riots happened almost daily and threats were made against my life. You don't scare me!" About three minutes passed and he appeared again and said, "You're all set; you can go back to work." A friend of mine was taking hers for her job in another agency at about the same time. She had to take the exam three times because her results kept coming back as inconclusive. I asked her, "What are you *doing* in there?" She is the type of person who likes to provide details and explain herself, so she wasn't just answering with a simple yes or no; she was giving more fuel for the polygrapher to doubt her, and made herself look guilty for nothing. On her last try, I told her to just answer yes or no and to keep her mouth shut otherwise. She passed!

The results of a polygraph will always be inconclusive because a polygraph cannot accurately detect deception. If spies can pass a polygraph test, why is it still in use? I find it a bit antiquated. Yes, the polygraph detects stress and anxiety; after all, it measures heartbeat, pulse, muscle tension, and even sweat. I also agree that for those people who get nervous and anxious when they lie, a polygraph can be a great tool for detecting deception, but again, never with 100-percent accuracy. So what's a polygrapher to do?

In my opinion, every polygrapher should be trained in what I know: how to accurately read the body to detect deceptive tells, and how to use questioning and elicitation techniques to extract truthful information. We should be using polygraphers who are also trained in body language to administer polygraphs so they can identify the verbal and nonverbal deceptive tells as the machine identifies stress. When such polygraphers see possible signs of deception, they can then use their training in questioning and elicitation to try to extract the truth, thus confirming the lie. By doing so they increase their odds of catching a spy, because the people taking the test not only have to beat the machine, they have to beat the polygrapher, and that will be harder. I think polygraphers hold the power to detecting deception, but I doubt the machine by itself does. If Anna Montes and the others had been interviewed by a polygrapher trained in body language and advanced interviewing techniques, the chances of them having been caught would have greatly increased.

Can we legally use advanced interviewing techniques on accused spies? We sure can! I train law enforcement personnel, arson investigators, and even auditors to conduct advanced, strategic interviews to legally and lawfully get the truth. As an interrogator I never put my detainees on a polygraph, because I didn't think it was a reliable tool for detecting deception. I had more faith in *my* ability to do that. However, I will share a secret with you: My detainees were under the impression—through the media, I suppose—that the polygraph machine was a piece of advanced technology that was precisely accurate in detecting lies. I didn't try to disabuse them of that notion; instead, I used it to my advantage, often by scheduling a polygraph as a ruse to see whether they were telling me the truth. The ruse played upon their fear of the unknown, which is a popular technique among interrogators. People generally fear what they do not know, and look to others for consolation when they are afraid. And before you start to think that this violates the Geneva Convention, know this: If a detainee has a fear, even something as slight as a concern, and it can be attributed to nothing but his own way of thinking, then he alone is responsible for this fear or uncertainty, and no one else. The fear of the unknown can crop up when you're meeting the in-laws for the first time, speaking in public for the first time, visiting a foreign country for the first time, riding a rollercoaster for the first time, starting a new job, or joining the military and being sent off to boot camp. In GTMO my detainees had fear—whether perceived, imagined, or real—of what would happen to them in their new, unfamiliar environment. Although we had strict schedules to ensure they were properly fed, bathed, exercised, and rested, they didn't always know this schedule, especially upon their arrival. I became the person who could also give them the answers to their fears; I reassured them as to what was going to happen on a day-to-day basis while they were in GTMO.

Fear is a powerful emotion. I took a Navy correspondence course while I was in the military titled "Captivity: The Extreme Circumstance." It was about Vietnam prisoners of war (POWs) who had survived life in captivity. What stood out to me most while taking that course was the fact that they claimed that the *fear* of torture was far greater than the torture itself. The reason is that they couldn't imagine how they would be tortured and the pain it would cause but once they were tortured and the pain came, there was no more guessing about what they would have to endure; therefore they could cope with it in the present moment, even though their treatment was beyond cruel and inhumane.

At GTMO, detainees' fear of the unknown allowed me to build rapport, gain their trust, and become their confidant, and this let me to collect intelligence information. How does this relate to the polygraph? I realized that they feared that the polygraph machine would tell me they were lying. So even though I have no confidence in a polygraph machine, I used their "fear of the polygraph" to my advantage. Often I would say, "If you are uncomfortable being hooked up to a machine that measures your breathing and your heart rate—all things you can't control when you lie—then I won't schedule one. But you'll have to tell me what really happened." Some people may wonder whether that could be looked at as a form of coercion. The definition of coercion is using force or threats to persuade someone to do something, so no, it was not applicable here. Having my detainees take a polygraph test wasn't a threat; it was a standard procedure available to interrogators to test the truthfulness in detainees, just as I was tested for truthfulness as a government employee. Their fear of this machine was no doing of mine, but it certainly worked to my advantage.

When you take a polygraph test you are only required to answer yes or no, so if you're trying to lie, you had better hope the questions are vaguely phrased. Take, for example, a question like this one: "Do you have any foreign contacts?" In this case the person or organization ordering the test wants to know if a foreign government is paying me, the test-taker, for U.S. information, and so I would answer no. But that question is vague, because who knows what they mean by "foreign contacts"? I have friends and colleagues who are Nigerian, South American, and German. So if I answer no but I am thinking of my Nigerian colleague, my cortisol may start to dispense, causing the polygraph machine's needle to move more rapidly and then—guess what?—I'm pegged as a liar. Obviously this is an exaggeration, as I am sure there is a margin of error with the machine. The machine has to baseline you, just as body-language experts do. It also has to take into account the stress people have just from taking the test. However, if I focus too much on my Nigerian colleague and worry that my answer will show signs of deception, it could *look* as though I were lying.

This is the same situation I talked about in Chapter 1, where I explain the problem with the old method of reading body language. Just because someone shrugs her shoulders as she states, "I don't know what happened to the money you left on the counter," doesn't mean she's lying and really knows where the money is. There could be other things on her mind, such as her dwindling bank account and the check she just bounced. So how can the polygraph machine and the polygrapher discriminate between ordinary stress, caused by a stressful situation, and stress caused by a lie? It can't. This is precisely why I believe that people are more accurate when it comes to detecting deception. Only people can look for multiple tells and stress indicators, and probe the topic(s) of conversation concurrent to the tell(s). Polygraphers have a predetermined line of questioning they need to get through, and most can't pursue a new line of questioning if they observe a shift in stress levels. At the end of the day, you need a human to probe into why there is stress.

Moreover, trained body-language experts can see physiological responses to stress in the body without the use of a polygraph machine. We can see people flushing, sweating, or turning pale; veins bulging; spit pooling in the mouth; hard swallowing; rapid eye blinking; and much more. The advantage of being a human lie detector is that we baseline people's normal behavior when they are comfortable first, so that we can see at what point in the conversation the tells appear. We also study the entire body from the head to the feet for facial micro-expressions, gestures, postures, and poses, as we conduct statement analysis simultaneously. I'd like to know what polygraph machine is able to do all that. So why are polygraph machines admissible in court, and human lie detectors aren't? Maybe it's because people trust a machine more than they trust other people.

Here is a case study submitted to me by a doctoral candidate at Henley Putnam University who agreed to let me share his story in this book regarding the inaccuracy of polygraphs when used to detect deception. The date, time, names, and circumstances have all been changed to protect the confidentiality of all involved:

> On, or about, 10 March 2014, Investigator Mike Smith initiated a criminal investigation against Joe, who told Mike that he had killed a man prior to joining the U.S. Army and threw the deceased in a ditch and buried him. Although the statements were made a year earlier, prior to Joe's deployment, Mike felt it was time to come forward to his command with the information that Joe disclosed to him, after observing Joe's concerning behavior while on deployment. Apparently, other individuals reported that Joe had made numerous threats against them and exhibited behavior consistent with psychopathy while on deployment as well. Because a year had gone by since Joe disclosed to Mike that he killed someone, Mike's command challenged Mike on his statement and the investigation he wanted to open against Joe. His command even accused Mike of lying about what Joe had said a year earlier. Joe had reportedly been present in many places where people had been killed during numerous battles while deployed. When questioned about the deaths and situations on the battlefield, Joe commented that he was not involved in the killings, but knew about the situations.

Initially, Joe's statements didn't make an impact on Mike, but as time went on and more and more issues arose regarding Joe's behavior, Mike started to take all this information very seriously and became very concerned about Joe's psychological stability. Joe even admitted to Mike that he had stalked a coworker with the intent to kill that individual for the perceived notion [that he or she had ruined] his career. Although to Mike the evidence was piling up against Joe's psychological instability, Joe was very popular among his peers, with many friends in high places who were willing to collude with him to protect him. Because of this, Mike's chain of command forced him to undergo a mental evaluation in hopes to prove Mike was just paranoid and had fabricated the entire situation.

In preparation for the mental evaluation, Mike underwent two other mental evaluations covertly, which were both favorable, in an effort to verify that he was not unstable in the event that the doctor agreed with the command and found him to be unstable and paranoid, [thereby] discrediting the investigation. He also personally paid for a polygraph test in order to further validate his statements.

Due to the extreme duress and pressure associated with the polygraph test, Mike Smith showed a 99.97 percent probability that he was lying about the issues surrounding Joe. Although Mike Smith vehemently claimed he was speaking the truth about the allegations, the stress of being hooked up to a polygraph machine that held the fate of his future, made his test results indicate he was not being truthful.

Having knowledge about polygraph tests and how they measure the physiological changes in the body when it's stressed, Mike commented to the polygraph expert administering the exam that the results were not surprising considering the level of stress he was under, not only from being hooked up to wires that measured his breathing and heart rate, but also from the stress his command was putting on him for not believing in him.

The polygraph expert attempted to convince Mike before and after that only dishonest people have heightened physiological responses to questions and that polygraphs are meant to pick up on this difference between the stress of taking a polygraph exam and the stress associated with lying. Mike confronted the polygraph expert about the many psychopaths who routinely pass polygraph exams as well as the many spies throughout history who have passed the test. The polygraph expert had no response other than to stand firm regarding the accuracy of the exam and was surprised that Mike did not take the test or the results seriously.

Fortunately for Mike, the polygraph test was not utilized in the case, and the investigation ensued against Joe; the investigation is still ongoing. The only reason Mike took the test is that he thought it might help absolve him of the false allegations made against him. Mike knew that people tend to believe in polygraph results, but taking the polygraph test only confirmed to him that it was not a reliable tool to detect deception. There is a belief among many in the profession that liars have elevated responses to lies and that normal people feel better when they tell the truth and do not have a fight or flight response when they are not lying. These [...] beliefs may be true in a significant number of cases; however, it is nowhere close to absolute. The problem is that the polygraph does not assess the possibility that under extreme duress, a participant may show elevated responses picked up by the polygraph when [he or she is] actually telling the truth.

—Anonymous PhD candidate at Henley Putnam
University

The New Polygraph?

Now you understand the complications and limitations that come along with using a polygraph as a lie detector machine. As of this writing two companies, No Lie MRI, Inc. and Cephos Corporation, both launched in 2006, have sought to address this by doing research on using functional magnetic resonance imaging (fMRI) to detect lies. These two companies are marketing fMRI as a deception-detecting method available to the public for use in legal proceedings, employment screening, and national security investigations, just to name a few. Many people are already questioning whether the fMRI is reliable or even ethical.

If you've never had an MRI, you are missing out on the enjoyment of lying in a very small tube, as motionless as possible, for 30 minutes, listening to a series of pounding and clicking noises and trying not to panic as you are stuck in the tight space. Not a fun experience for those who are claustrophobic! MRIs use a powerful magnetic field and radio frequency pulses to produce detailed images of the interior structures of our bodies. FMRI is a rather recent development in magnetic resonance technology that allows doctors to see "functional" images of the brain, not just the structure of the brain. It does this by measuring blood flow in the brain. Because of this, scientists (using fMRI) have been able to pinpoint regions of the brain that change when a person lies, called *regions of deceit*. When activity in these areas increases, so does the blood flow:

> Even without a clear "lying" region, researchers can use fMRI to detect when a study participant is telling a lie in the laboratory with about 85-percent accuracy.... Even with such a high rate of accuracy, however, use of fMRI and polygraph tests to identify deceit outside of the laboratory is controversial" (source: *Society for Neuroscience*).

Although not yet deemed admissible in U.S. or European courts, the fMRI has already been used in court as evidence in India, and has also been used on the British reality TV show *Lie Lab*. While fMRI boasts greater accuracy than the polygraph, neuroscientists Anthony

Wagner of Stanford University and Giorgio Ganis of the University of Plymouth say there isn't enough evidence to support the use of fMRI for lie detection. The scientific community has also raised the concern about whether or not the use of this technology could be abused and violates individual rights. However, these concerns can be said of the polygraph, as well. When you compare the two methods, all other factors being equal, a polygraph and polygrapher are much easier to transport to a courtroom or detention center in some remote location, and certainly they are more cost effective. We'll have to wait to see what the future holds for the role of fMRI in detecting deception. In the meantime, we can still rely on our body-language experts with a great deal of confidence.

As a former interrogator, I used my detecting deception skills while deployed to GTMO working in the detainee prison interrogating members of the Taliban and al Qaeda to gather intelligence to save lives, and those skills worked. In my opinion, in the world of detecting deception, cops, interrogators, attorneys, judges, investigators, and even human resource personnel are far better off using a human lie detector to get to the truth than they are with a machine that can only detect stress. In the following chapters I will teach you how to *accurately* detect deception and be able to decipher the difference between deceptive tells in deceitful people and perceived deceptive tells in truthful people. Only after being trained in advanced techniques such as these can you detect deception accurately—not with 100-percent accuracy (unless you are a truth wizard!), but pretty close to it. After all, what better tool is there to get into the mind of human than another human?

4

My Five-Step Program for Reading Body Language: Be a Body-Language Expert; Be a REBLE

The REBLE program is an easy-to-follow, five-step program I created to spot lies and get to the truth. REBLE is an acronym that stands for **R**elax, **E**stablish rapport, **B**aseline behavior, **L**ook for deviations from the baseline, and **E**xtract the truth. I like the word "rebel" because according to Urban Dictionary, it means "a person who stands up for his or her own personal opinions despite what anyone else says. A true rebel stands up for what he or she believes is right, not against what's right." I believe that everyone should have the courage to stand up for themselves, speak their minds, and do what they think is right. I didn't always have the courage to do this when I was younger, but I do now. And once you have it, you'll never lose it; in fact, your courage and confidence will only get stronger. If only the poor kids who are being bullied today had the courage and confidence to be able to say "Whatever!" to cowardly bullies, they would defeat them and walk away with their heads held high.

Kelly O'Clair, a friend and colleague of mine, and I are currently brainstorming a program to empower teenagers and adults who are being bullied at school and in the office. People of all ages and backgrounds can use the power of body language. My REBLE program is meant for anyone who wants to:

- Build amazing rapport and relationships with people.
- Win trust and gain respect.

53

- Have the courage to stand up for themselves.
- Confront those who are deceiving them or their loved ones.
- Never be a victim of mental or physical abuse.
- Never be taken advantage of or caught in a scam.
- Have the confidence to go after what they want: that new job, a promotion, a new romantic interest, whatever.
- Determine whether someone is lying to them.
- Get the truth while maintaining rapport and respect.
- Collect accurate and truthful information.

The REBLE body-language program isn't just about detecting deception, honing in on verbal and nonverbal deceptive tells, and getting to the truth; it's also about finding your confidence and building strong, healthy relationships and connections with people. You will learn how to build rapport with people and how to assess their personality preferences so you can adjust yours to meet theirs. You will learn that people tend to like other people who are similar to them. You will also learn that most people inherently want to be honest— even terrorists and criminals! In fact, when my detainees "broke" (when they finally gave up resisting and told the truth), every one of them said the same thing to me: "It's such a relief to not have to lie anymore." People want to be respected *and* feel good about themselves; knowing this was partly why I was so successful as an interrogator. Yes, I used all the approach techniques I was taught, as well as my analytical and questioning skills, but I also focused on the human factor. I forced myself to look at every single detainee, no matter what his background was or what he had done, as a human being first. It wasn't easy, but I knew if I could show them respect as fellow human beings, even though I abhorred what they did, they would reciprocate that respect. (I admit that sometimes that was really difficult. I would feel the corners of my mouth turn down in disgust while talking to them, and then quickly try to smile, hoping they didn't see the micro-expression leaking out of my face.) I got respect and, more importantly, a lot of important intelligence information out of them. Not all interrogators, especially tactical interrogators, agree with or follow my method, but for the strategic interrogation environment, where I had the time to build relationships, my method worked well. Being a nonthreatening female also worked to my advantage.

My program debunks the prevailing myths about reading body language, such that even the naysayers will want to incorporate this program into their everyday lives. I use this program. It works. I used it with the detainees at Guantanamo Bay, and even though I had no "program" for what I was doing in the interrogation booth at the time, I knew that I was succeeding. And, of course, I've used it to start my own company, The Congruency Group. We live in a big, complex world, and unfortunately there are a lot of bad people out there who have bad intentions to harm others. I know, because I've seen many of these people up close. Use my five-step body-language program to take control of your life and protect yourself and those close to you from being hurt, let down, taken advantage of, or deceived.

5

R Is for Relax

The first step in the REBLE program is to relax. A big part of this will involve cultivating some self-awareness. Before you can begin to read other people you have to know what your own body is saying. For example, when I was interrogating detainees in GTMO, do you think for one minute they would have given me information if I looked scared, incompetent, or dishonest? Remember that the only way to look confident is to feel confident. How is your body posture right now, as you are reading this book? Are you slouched over with your shoulders rolled inward and your chin down? Or do you have your chest puffed out, your shoulders back, and your chin up? Are you sitting with your ankles crossed, or with one leg crossed over the other knee in a figure four? Do you look confident and self-assured, or timid and unsure? When people look confident, they are likely feeling relaxed and calm. When people look unsure of themselves, they are likely feeling uncomfortable and nervous. You need to understand how to look relaxed in order to get to the next step in my five-step program: establish rapport. No one will want to even talk to you, let alone build rapport with you, if you look tense or skittish.

Failure and Acceptance

Feeling confident about who you are takes some time and some acceptance of your life traveled thus far. We have all heard the saying

"If at first you don't succeed, try, try again." Don't give up, even after you experience failure. We all have and will continue to stumble, but you must learn to experience and embrace failure, because ultimately it will lead to your success. I am speaking from firsthand experience on this subject, and I'm sure you can, too. When we fail at something, a lot of negative emotions are associated with that failure: shame, guilt, fear, doubt, inadequacy, embarrassment, unworthiness, nervousness, and even grief. After failing at a task, a mission, a goal, or an assignment, you may think those around you will always remember you for your failure; you may feel that you've lost credibility permanently, which ultimately erodes your self-confidence. We tend to be our own worst critics. Other people forgive our mistakes far more easily than we can forgive ourselves.

I'm going to share a couple of failures I have experienced in my life and tell you what happened right after each one. My first story goes back in time to my college years. The four years I spent working toward my bachelor's degree were divided into two majors: accounting, following Dad's footsteps and failing miserably, resulting in being put on probation; and anthropology, which got me on the Dean's List. I wish then I understood why I failed at accounting so I wouldn't have thought I was just stupid. At that time I was being groomed to take over my dad's successful CPA business, but I had no idea that I had a learning style preference, or that there even was such a thing. I had a heart-to-heart with my father, explaining that numbers drove me mad and that understanding mathematical equations was like trying to read Greek. (Actually, I learned to read and speak Greek years later, and it was a breeze!) What I didn't realize was that I was and am an "Intuitive" (according to Jungian personality preferences); I take in a process information conceptually, I follow my inspiration, and I imagine possibilities for the future. I hated rules, deadlines, details, and processes. Tell me to create a new theory on cross-cultural communication? I was all over it. Tell me to balance a checkbook? I would wallow in frustration and defeat. My dad, on the other hand, takes in information as a "Sensor";

he enjoys factual, detail-oriented information and prefers to have rules, instructions, and processes. This way of being and approaching the world makes sense to him and it's easy for him, which is why he gravitated toward the field of accounting and is a very successful CPA. I also realized I wasn't stupid. So I decide to change majors to anthropology and archaeology, even though I had no clue where was I going to find a job "digging rocks," as my dad would say. But I was in heaven, loving what I was learning and excelling in all my classes.

After I graduated with a BA in anthropology, I decided with my newfound confidence to apply to Brown University for graduate school. I still don't know how or why, but I was accepted. It was probably one of the biggest challenges in my life, but I didn't let it scare me; I was ready to jump in! I ended up falling on my face, quite a few times, but I always got back up again. During those two long years I experienced failure more than a few times. For example, during an art history lecture, my professor called on me to discuss a question. I will never forget what happened next. I became so nervous that my body started doing things I couldn't control. (Now, of course, I know why: It was the physiological response to the cortisol, that pesky stress hormone, being released in my body.) My voice trembled, the pitch of my voice went up, my hands shook like crazy, and I started swallowing hard because my mouth suddenly felt like it was filled with cotton. I fell apart. I was so humiliated. *Why am I so scared of people? It's ridiculous,* I thought. I was terrified of looking stupid in front of people, and of course I did just that. Although no one let on, I knew that everyone had seen me lose it. I got so mad at and down on myself that I felt as though I didn't belong there. The incident played in my mind over and over all night long.

When I woke up the next day, I was no longer humiliated and embarrassed; I was angry. Now I was on a mission to prove to that class—and to myself—that not only did I know the material, but I could present it professionally and eloquently. I wasn't going to let a professor and a handful of students scare me! When our end-of-semester class presentations came around, I volunteered to go first. There was no way I was letting that last horrible impression of myself linger. I knew I had it in me and I was determined they were going to see me confidently present for two hours on my topic. I even put more pressure on myself by using dual slide shows running simultaneously (this was 1995, so we didn't have the technology we have today). I gave the best presentation I had given in my life up to that point. I was so happy with myself that I barely noticed I was getting a standing ovation for my presentation. The day I fell apart never haunted me again; in fact, I was thankful for the strength and confidence I found in myself because of it. Of course it didn't cure my insecurities, and I still felt them from time to time during the next year and a half, but it certainly was a huge stepping-stone and learning opportunity for me that I will never forget or regret. I overcame my fear by forcing myself to appear, act, and feel confident, and you can, too.

Why am I sharing this with you? To prove to you that I am the best example of my theory that once you act and hence feel confident, you can conquer your greatest fear. Did you know that the most common fear is the fear of public speaking? It's not a life-or-death situation, yet it is the number-one most fear for most people. The fear of failure and shame, based on how others perceive us, is very powerful. America is a society of guilt; some countries in the Middle East are societies of shame. Guilt, shame, and embarrassment cause us fear, and that fear is just as crippling as when our lives are being threatened. You're going to need confidence to use the tools in this book and use them successfully. If I have confidence in you to use them, you need to do your part and find it. Deal? So don't worry about failing or screwing up. We all do in some form or another. When it happens, learn from it instead of getting down on yourself. Every human being on this planet will fail at something, at some point, so you are not alone.

Here are a few of my favorite quotes about confidence. Hopefully you'll find them encouraging, too:

- "Confidence doesn't come from always being right; it comes from not fearing to be wrong." (Peter T. Mcintyre)
- "If you are going to doubt something, doubt your limits." (Don Ward)
- "People who say it cannot be done should not interrupt those who are doing it." (George Bernard Shaw)
- "True confidence is the mentor; professed confidence is the aggressor." (That one's mine.)

A former colleague of mine—we'll call him Jack—took a senior position a bit outside his comfort zone. Jack was liked by many and had a good work ethic; he was also a mentor to junior employees and an enthusiastic team player. Until he stepped into a management position. Up until this point in his career Jack was "one of the guys" who had your back in tough times, but he hadn't held a managerial position before. Knowing he was a bit inexperienced didn't engender humility, unfortunately; it made him feel that he really had to prove himself in this position. It was good that he accepted the challenge, but bad that he became aggressive with those who worked with him.

He began to alienate his colleagues and friends by being brash, confrontational, and emotionally heated. He lost all sense of diplomacy. Once he was down in the trenches with his fellow soldiers; now he was barking commands from his throne. How did this new position change him from a person who everybody respected to a person everyone disrespected? You can probably guess. His lack of confidence in himself made him aggressive. He was mad at himself for not having the knowledge to hit the ground running in this new position and was worried that people would see that he didn't have all the answers—which would have been okay! But he thought he would lose respect if he asked for advice. What he didn't know is that he would have gotten *more* respect if he had done that, not less. His anger and worry turned him authoritative to the point of being disrespectful; it was all a smokescreen to get people to think he was confident. Thankfully for Jack, those who knew him overlooked his displays of aggression. You have probably seen people who compensate for lack of confidence the same way. Or maybe you are one of these yourself. They equate being bossy and aggressive with confidence, when it's actually a telltale sign of quite the opposite. Look at Anthony Weiner and Lance Armstrong and how condescending, confrontational, and even aggressive they were to the press prior to admitting their lies. They were both trying to convince the public of their lies and they did so by bullying those around them.

Another experience I'd like to share with you that's relevant to feeling relaxed and confident happened to me when I joined the Military Reserves and experienced personal failure, again, to the point I was so disappointed in myself that I had no other choice but to conquer my fear. But this time the consequences were far worse than having a bunch of graduate students see me get a case of stage fright. I had just been mobilized for one year of active duty service and was being trained as a certified Department of Defense (DoD) interrogator. Basically I had been sent on a trip to the Caribbean island of Cuba, where I stayed at a .5-star resort surrounded by tourists—I mean terrorists—eating gourmet cuisine that came conveniently wrapped up all in one package. I knew I was not in Rhode Island anymore.

When I arrived I had exactly one day to get my housing assignment, check in, and learn the lay of the land. The next day I went to the prison where I would be working every day, to get a turnover from the team I was relieving and a tour of the camp. As I was escorted to the trailers we used as interrogation booths, the guard opened the door and an overwhelming smell of sweat, urine, and vomit covered up by lemon air freshener hit me in the face as I stood in the hot sun. I wanted to turn around and run, but obviously I couldn't. This was where I would be interrogating for the next five months for hours on end. *How the hell am I going to work in this stench?* I wondered.

The day finally came when I was scheduled to interrogate my very first detainee. When I was attending interrogation training in 1999, I never thought I was actually going to use my training in "real life." Here was my chance. I met my interpreter at 0800 hours in my office, which turned out to be a small room in a trailer identical to the interrogation booth trailer, and we walked through three sally ports (secure controlled entryways to the prison) and past military guards escorting detainees in shackles to our destination: Yellow Trailer, Booth #7. During our walk I pre-briefed the interpreter I was to work with that day on how the interrogation was going to unfold. I told him how I was going to build rapport with the detainee, the topics I was going to question him on, the incentive items I was going to offer the detainee, where I wanted of all us to sit, when we would take breaks, how long we were going to be in the interrogation, and so on. In short, I had a plan. Yellow Trailer had about eight interrogation booths inside, buffered by observation booths on each side with two-way mirrors, one control booth at the entryway containing guards and video equipment, and a *head*, or latrine (depending on what branch of service you are in). As we waited in Booth #7 I heard the door open to the trailer and a guard shout, "Detainee on deck!" (GTMO is a Navy base; *deck* is the floor in Navy talk.) *Here's my guy,* I thought. *A real detainee.* When the guards escorted detainees to their interrogation booths everyone had to stay in their rooms; no one was allowed to be in the hallway for security reasons. I heard the clanking of the chains around his feet getting closer and the heavy shuffling of his footsteps. I had no idea what he was going to look like. Would he be fierce and belligerent and fight the guards? Or would he be docile and weep once seated in the chair? My heart leaped into my chest. I felt my pulse quicken and pound in my head. I started to doubt my plan. Maybe I should stand, or sit, or move the furniture; or maybe I should have come in after the detainee.

Too late now—there he was at the door. The guards stopped him and asked me if it was okay to enter. I said yes and saw this this thin, messy-haired man in a bright orange jump suit and flip-flops enter the room. He looked at me and rolled his eyes. *Great.* I already felt defeated, because with that eye roll, he had the upper hand within a second. For the next hour I asked questions and got vague answers.

I couldn't build rapport, and he would not maintain eye contact. I could tell from his body language that he thought the whole thing was a joke. I felt humiliated. After only two hours I terminated the interrogation and sent him back to his cell. The interpreter and I walked back to my office, but I felt as though I was doing the walk of shame. *What the hell am I doing here? I can't do this*, I said to myself. Not only did I feel like a failure, but, even worse, I was letting my fellow military members on the front lines down because I didn't get any information out of that guy. I sent him back to his cell because I gave up. I didn't sleep at all that night.

That next morning I had another interrogation at 0800 with a different detainee but with the same interpreter. The interpreter met me at 0730; he was an older man, very pleasant and nice, with a great, upbeat attitude. I thought to myself, *You're not going to see the same loser girl you did yesterday!* That day he was going to see the real me, the confident, high-energy, quick-witted girl who scrutinizes every single body movement and every single word coming out of someone's mouth, and who enjoys mental sparring to get to truth. I stood tall took a deep breath and said to myself, *Bring it on*. The next eight hours went by in the blink of an eye. I had pages and pages of notes. I had to end the interrogation so that the detainee and my interpreter could eat. I wasn't even hungry, I was on such a high. That day on the walk back to my office I walked with my head held high. Never again would I allow a detainee make me doubt my ability or get the upper hand. I knew what I was capable of doing; it just took a little bit of anger to get past my fear of the unknown, find my confidence, and relax into this new environment. Right before we entered our offices my interpreter patted me on my shoulder and said, "That was impressive. I'd like to request to work with you while you are here." And that was the start of my many follow-on successes at GTMO. In fact I had to beg my command to stay another month because I didn't want to leave. The Commanding General of GMTO told my home command that I was "an asset here" and requested me to stay another month. I stayed. Oh, and when new interrogators would arrive and get the VIP tour of the prison and the interrogations booths, they would always ask me, "How do you stand that smell?" I would reply, "What smell?"

Are you starting to see a trend? It took failure and disappointment in myself to give me the inner strength to find my confidence and accomplish my goals, whether it was giving a killer presentation or getting intelligence information from detainees. I can look back now and view those two events as negative experiences with positive outcomes. Deep down, I knew I had the skills, knowledge, finesse, determination, and confidence; I just needed some help bringing it out. I found out how to relax and gain confidence, and I know you can do the same.

Think of a time in your life when you felt shame, embarrassment, and/or disappointment in your actions. Write down what happened and how you felt. What did you do afterward? What will you do if and when something like this happens again?

No one can make you confident; only you can. The question you need to ask yourself is: Are you willing to give up the fear of failure and challenge yourself to bring out your inner confidence? We all have it! I'm going to help you with this challenge by giving you some pointers on how you can tap into your inner confident you. These pointers will also be in your toolkit and checklist at the end of the book.

What Happens to the Body Under Stress

So let's talk more about what actually happens inside the body when we become stressed, nervous, or anxious. My students used to ask me all the time, "How do I stop from being nervous?" I tell them exactly what I'm going to tell you; you have to *not* be nervous. Nothing like stating the obvious, right? Unfortunately, there is nothing you can do to stop the hypothalamus from causing the release of the stress hormone cortisol that we talked about in Chapter 2, or to prevent your body from responding physiologically as a result, at least not until the perceived threat or fear has passed. You have to learn to manage your emotions *before* you get to that state. Without getting too scientific I'm going to briefly explain the science behind what happens when the body is trying to protect itself when it perceives a threat.

Once a threat is identified and fear is established (and remember that a "threat" can be public speaking, not just being chased by a wild animal), the body goes into a fight-or-flight response; do you stay and fight the threat, or do you run away and evade it? Imagine that you are just about to go on stage, and even though you know your material inside and out, all of a sudden your heart starts pounding and your breathing becomes more rapid and shallow. The adrenal glands, located on top of your kidneys, release a surge of hormones that include adrenaline and cortisol. Adrenaline is released into your body when you feel stressed. You can feel the effects of it immediately; it increases your heart rate, elevates your blood pressure, and boosts immediate energy supplies. Another hormone that is released, *norepinephrine* (also called *noradrenaline*), focuses your attention and sharpens your senses. Then the stress hormone cortisol is released. These three hormones—adrenaline, norepinephrine, and cortisol—give you the heightened energy, focused attention, and sharpened senses you need to fight or escape a threat. Cortisol's mechanism is a bit more complicated to explain, and does a host of things to maintain the stability, or *homeostasis*, of the human body while responding to external stimuli. For example, during stressful situations, cortisol can temporarily increase your immunity, increase your blood sugar (making sure that both the brain and the body have enough fuel to function at these heightened levels), and suppress non-essential bodily functions during flight or fight, such as digesting or excreting. Think about the last time you were in a high-stress situation. Did you feel hunger and have to eat to maintain your energy? Probably not.

As adrenaline pumps through your body, you may be able to run faster and even become stronger. Have you seen those stories of housewives who have been able to lift up a car by themselves when someone was trapped underneath it? That's adrenaline. The rush of norepinephrine will heighten your senses; you'll be able to see better in the dark, and your sense of smell will be extra keen. You'll even be able to smell fear, a pungent, unmistakable odor that is a mix of a metallic smell and body odor, and something I smelled often while I was interrogating in GTMO. (Some people don't believe me when I say I have smelled fear, but ask any military member who's been in combat, any cop, any firefighter, or any interrogator if they have ever smelled fear; most know it well, and will be able to recognize it a mile away.) And finally, cortisol will tap into the energy stores in your body (fat) to provide energy where the body needs it most, such as the large muscles in your legs and arms, to help you fight or run away from the threat. The boost of energy you get from these hormones may even shock you at times. Because your brain doesn't "know" why you are nervous, it treats the stress from public speaking and stress from being chased by someone with a gun the same way.

Dr. Mary Gardner, veterinarian and cofounder of the Lap of Love, says that when animals get stressed their bodies go through a process called SLUDD, an acronym that stands for salivate, lacrimate (watering eyes), urinate, digest, and defecate. These symptoms are called *parasympathetic* symptoms and they regulate body functions such as heart rate, digestion, excretion, and even sexual functions. In animals, SLUDD is what happens as a consequence of the animal preparing its organs for stress, and corresponds to how our bodies prepare for fight or flight. That's the basic science behind why your hands shake, your voice quivers, you start to sweat, your heart pounds, and you feel as though you could leap tall buildings in a single bound, when you get nervous or feel threatened.

We all have fears and anxieties, so how can we overcome them? By convincing our brain there is no perceived threat. How can you do that? By convincing your brain you are confident, calm, and in control—relaxed. Believe it or not, you can do this by positioning your body in a certain way, in what I call *power poses*. Don't worry, this doesn't involve doing yoga poses, although I do recommend it to relieve stress and feel energized.

Confidence Body Gestures: Do's and Don'ts

Hooking and the thumbs of power

Remember when your mother would admonish you to stand up straight? She probably didn't realize she was telling you to look and feel more confident. Changing your posture can actually change the way you feel about yourself. When you observe authority figures, people you respect and admire, whether at work, at home, or in the media, take notice of their body posture. How do they typically stand and present themselves? By contrast, if you look at a photo of Woody Allen, he is typically seen slumped over, with his shoulders rolled forward, his chin tucked in, and his eyes looking down at the ground. Now look at any photo of James Dean; he probably looks like the exact opposite of Woody Allen. Check out his posture, his shoulders, his chest, his chin, and his eye contact. There's a reason why women swooned over James Dean and not Woody Allen. Can you guess why? It's not so much their looks as it is their display of confidence. Guys always say that "good guys come in last" or "girls don't want a good guy"—well, guys, you're wrong. We all want a good guy, but we want that good guy to be a *confident* guy. Good guys can be confident, too. Just remember: James Dean oozed confidence, but Woody Allen does not.

Both Woody Allen and James Dean have been photographed in a *hooking* pose, with their hands in their pockets or waist bands, and their thumbs at an angle, pointing toward their private parts, or "naughty bits," as the British say. James Dean has sex appeal when he does this. Woody Allen—not so much. The reason is the

The Woody Allen hooking pose.   *The James Dean hooking pose.*

difference in their posture. Look at the following two images. Can you see the difference?

In the image on the left you can see my model, Kelly, standing in the Woody Allen hooking pose. His shoulders are down, slumped forward, and curled inward; his eyes are looking straight ahead; and his chin is tucked in. He looks as though he were ready to curl up in a ball and hide from the world. In the image on the right, Kelly is standing in a wide stance, with his feet about 10 to 12 inches apart. He has good posture, his shoulders are back, he maintains good eye contact with the camera, and his chin is lifted; he looks as though he were ready to take on the world. Change your stance, gentlemen, and you will change both how you feel *and* how others feel about you. Start doing this now! If you are a nice guy, and I hope you are, stand like this and you will get the girls; you will win in the end because eventually, girls leave the bad guys (or at least they should).

So why do guys frame their private parts, anyway? It's as obvious as you think: It's meant to communicate male sexuality. Male
private parts are a symbol of male virility and power. How many
times have you seen sexy bad boys on TV or in the movies assume
this pose, and women can't resist them? When males *hook*, or frame,
their private parts, it signifies that they are a sexual threat and is
meant to intimidate other men. It's similar to the way in which a
gorilla beats its chest to show strength and dominance and intimidate other male gorillas. When a guy hooks and positions one leg
slightly higher than the other—for example, putting it on a footrest
at a bar—he is subconsciously pushing out his private parts as a sign
of extreme confidence, almost as though he were saying, "Hey, look
at what I have to offer!" So why do women do it too? Both Angelina
Jolie and fashion model Amber LeBon have been photographed this
way. Are they trying to scare off male predators? No, they do it for
the same reason: to show confidence and display one of their three
vulnerable zones. If you expose your three vulnerable zones—your
neck dimple, your belly, and your groin—you are subconsciously
saying to the world, "Bring it on. I can handle anything." It is display of power, and both girls and guys can display confidence and
power this way. Women, if a guy does this at a bar while he's staring
at you or talking to you, he's probably trying to impress you with
his, um, good looks and pick you up.

As a general rule I tell people never to hide their hands, because when you hide your hands, you hide your emotions, and you
will look insincere and untrustworthy. However, if you have to put
your hands in your pockets, keep your thumbs out. As a modi-
fied phallic symbol, the thumb symbolizes power, and displaying
the thumbs for all to see is a sign of confidence. I call exposing or
displaying the thumbs in this way the "thumbs of power" because
it's a gesture of confidence, however subtle. You may not have noticed this, but when you are feeling strong and confident, the space
between your fingers actually grows, making your hands take up
more space. In essence they become more territorial. When you

The Fonz thumbs of power.

feel insecure, that space disappears; in fact, you may find your-self tucking your thumbs under your fingers or hiding your hands away completely. When you feel confident, your thumbs will tend to point upward as you speak. I have noticed over the years that when I get up and present, my thumbs are always sticking way out there, just like those of the Fonz! Who doesn't remember the Fonz from *Happy Days*? His signature move was to raise both of his fists with thumbs out and say, "Heeeey!" The Fonz oozed confidence, strutting around in that leather jacket, white t-shirt, and blue jeans, and at the snap of his fingers, chicks would flock to him. Obviously it was a TV show and they were actors, but don't you think there was a reason why the writer and director chose that body gesture to create the confident, chick-magnet image of the Fonz? Richie Cunningham never did that. The moment you hide your thumbs you're saying "I feel insecure; I need reassurance." Children hide their thumbs in their fists, and babies suck their thumbs because they feel insecure. As they grow older, most kids stop sucking their thumbs as they slowly become more confident in the world. I sincerely hope that you don't still suck your thumbs, but definitely stop hiding them!

This past News Year's Eve I was invited to a five-course wine pairing dinner with friends. Across the table from me sat this beautiful, bubbly girl whom I just met named Leslie. She was full of life, open, and friendly. Once she found out what I did, she leaned in across the table, lowered her voice, and asked me, "Can you help me deal with this girl in my office who is always out to get me? She is always condescending and putting me down." I replied, "I sure can." After I had her explain the situation, I told her the next time she was around this girl in her work environment, she needed to exhibit confidence through body poses and gestures, because once she looked confident, she would feel confident. Here are some body confidence poses—power poses—and gestures that you can use to look and feel confident.

Power poses and belly breathing

In a paper published in *Psychological Science,* Amy Cuddy (of Harvard Business School), and Dana R. Carney and Andy J. Yap (both of Columbia University) reported how they measured the hormone levels of 42 male and female research subjects 17 minutes after they were placed either in a high-power or low-power poses for a minute per pose. They concluded that a mere *two minutes* in a pose caused significant changes in testosterone and cortisol. The high-power poses lead to increased feelings of confidence and a higher tolerance for risk. The study also found that people are more often influenced by how they feel about another person than by what that person is saying.

Try this the next time you get up in front of a room full of people to speak, or sit down for a job interview, or have a heart-to-heart conversation with a loved one that you are nervous or anxious about. Assume a power pose; plant your feet into ground about 10 inches apart and take a deep breath from your stomach, not your chest. If you breathe with your diaphragm, you will lessen anxiety, anger, and the feeling of panic. Diaphragm breathing is called belly breathing, and has very different effects than rapid chest breathing. Unfortunately, we have evolved into being chest breathers. As a point of comparison, watch a newborn baby breathe. What is rising and falling? The stomach, not the chest. With societal expectations for thinness and fitness, we have started to breathe from our chests rather than our stomachs. Who wants to walk around expanding their stomach, right? We are too busy sucking them in! What most don't realize is that breathing from the stomach actually has a meditative, calming effect.

Back in the late 1990s, I wanted to lose weight and get on a health kick. I was tired of having a gut. Determined, I told myself I had to start running to lose weight, plain and simple. But up until that point as a 20-something, I had never run. I would get so nervous before I ran because I was worried I was going to collapse from being out of shape. So I started to run with really good posture to calm my erratic breathing (it was erratic from being completely out of shape and the resulting feeling of panic). I also ran with a band that weightlifters use to support their lower backs while lifting. This band actually helped support my posture and soon I was running outside in the middle of winter on a deserted beach in the dark three times a week, going farther and farther each time. The very first time I ran I barely ran a quarter of a mile before hyperventilating, but eventually I worked my way up to running five miles. How I got over the initial hump was all due to purposefully calming myself by having good posture and breathing deeply from my belly.

Another great power pose to take is the Wonder Woman or Superman pose. In both, you put your hands on your hips, with your feet about 10 inches apart, and stand with good posture. When your body is fully erect, your lungs and diaphragm can function better. Breathing deeply and calmly will start to transform how you feel; you will begin to feel calm and powerful. Trust me! Try it right now. While standing in this position I want you to think of a time when you felt your best, whether out of happiness or success. Take your time and think about what happened to cause to feel this way. Then mentally anchor those events to your body stance. Now that you have connected these positive thoughts and feelings to a power pose, every time you feel scared, nervous, weak, shy, or intimidated, go off somewhere by yourself and assume your power pose. Breathe deeply and think of your anchored thoughts of success and energy. Another good pose is the runner's victory stance. Raise and extend your arms up into the air and stretch as far as you can. Why do you think all athletes do this when they win? They all do it instinctively. It reaffirms and increases the feeling of being victorious and strong. But you don't have to be a world-class athlete do it!

I will warn you that assuming a power pose with others can come across as dominating and controlling. Be careful not to ruin rapport with someone by appearing superior to them; your purpose with this pose is to make *yourself* feel dominant, in control, and powerful. Also, avoid putting only one hand on your hip; you may think that this will help you appear confident but it actually sends a signal of disrespectfulness and defiance—that you are a know-it-all or you are about to lock horns with someone. If you want to look and feel confident, go with both hands on your hips. This is a positive, powerful pose.

Jodi Arias, one of my favorite recent criminal cases to analyze, assumed an extreme power pose the first time she was taken into custody and questioned by law enforcement personnel on July 15, 2008. This was after the body of her boyfriend, Travis Alexander, was found stabbed and shot in the shower in his home. In a YouTube video titled *Jodi Arias Unedited Police Interrogation Video 5*, she demonstrates some really odd behavior when she is left alone in the interrogation room where she was being recorded, unbeknownst to her. A detective enters to talk to her and reads her her rights. After they talk for a while he leaves, and she is left alone. You can hear he say out loud, "You should have at least done your makeup, Jodi. Gosh." Then she starts to sing, plays with a water bottle, looks in a garbage can, laughs and says something inaudible, flips her hair, preens her finger nails, puts her knees up, twirls her hair, and then does a headstand! Debbie Pokornik, author of *Standing in Your Power: A Guide for Living Your Life Fully Awake,* says that when you put your feet above your head, it signals the body that it is safe and hence focuses its energies on making you healthy. It can also help you relax and release pent-up emotions. Maybe that's why Jodi did one in the interrogation room. If you are emotional or lacking self-control and confidence, do a handstand. When I get super stressed or angry, to the point that my heart is palpitating and I am grabbing fists of my hair, I do handstand. After a few minutes I am calm as a still lake. Funny how that works!

Steepling

Steepling is another power pose. There are four ways to steeple: the regular church steeple (a Donald Trump favorite), the low steeple (an Oprah favorite), the handgun steeple (politicians' favorite), and the basketball steeple (my favorite). No matter which steeple you use, it says you are knowledgeable, confident, and self-assured. It will make you feel powerful and confident. However, be careful of knowing when to use a steeple because it can come across as aggressive and domineering, especially the handgun steeple; only use this one as a last resort because it can make you lose rapport quickly.

The church steeple: Place all of your fingertips together in the shape of a church steeple and hold your hands out in front of your chest, or rest them on a surface in front of you. Some of you may be intimately familiar with this steeple. You also may have been steepled by someone else—your boss, an interviewer, a superior, anyone in a position of greater power. When people are contemplating an issue or about to make a decision they often will use a church steeple to show they have the knowledge and authority to make that decision. In the following image you can see Kelly steepling as he has a conversation with Chris; he is unconsciously saying he has the power and is in control. Chris, on the other hand, has his arms folded in a defensive manner. Although crossing the arms doesn't always mean

The church steeple.

someone is defensive (it could just be that he is cold or thinking about something), here Chris has also leaned back, creating more distance between himself and Kelly. This tells me Chris is feeling more defensive than cold or contemplative. Be careful when you use the steeple; you may lose rapport and upset the other person. Although I highly recommend steepling a bully!

The low steeple: The low steeple is the same as a church steeple but your hands are lowered almost covering your private parts. This steeple is subtler than the high church steeple. It stills says you feel powerful but you aren't in shoving your confidence in people's faces. It a subtle way to say, I ultimately have the control but I am not beneath hearing what you have to say either.

The basketball steeple: To do the basketball steeple, open your hands as though you were holding an imaginary basketball out in front of you. (Extraverts will actually go wider than a basketball to make the gesture bigger and grander.) The basketball steeple is a

The low steeple.

The basketball steeple.

The resting handgun steeple.

likeable gesture and makes you appear powerful yet approachable. This is the most effective steeple to get others to believe in you; it says you are hopeful but firm in your convictions. I use this unconsciously when I speak, probably because I feel I am the authority on the subject matter I am speaking about, but instead of fearing me, I want the audience to like me. Many public speakers use the basketball steeple; it's a favorite gesture of President Barack Obama.

The handgun steeple: This steeple is downright aggressive. It says you mean business! The handgun steeple can be overbearing, controlling, and patronizing because you are unconsciously shooting down what other people say. In the image above you can see Kelly exhibiting a "resting handgun steeple", in which his chin is resting on his "handgun." Sometimes people rest the handgun steeple against their lips, which can be a sign of disapproval or deep thought, or an indication that an internal dialogue going on. It can also mean they are trying to keep their mouths shut. In the "shooting handgun

Hitler hands.

steeple" the handgun is actually aimed at someone. This version is really aggressive because it looks as though you subconsciously want to shoot the other person. The handgun steeple should never be used when seeking diplomacy or when seeking agreement among peers. It should only be used when deliberately trying to intimidate another individual or group.

Hitler hands

This palm-down gesture, with the arm extended straight out like the Nazi salute or Hitler salute, is reprimanding and authoritative. It subconsciously says "Pay attention to me, or else." I call this move "Hitler hands." It has a stifling effect on others as it negates or nullifies what they have just said. This gesture is condescending—parents yell at children this way—but if you really want the upper hand, put your palm down.

The palm push.

Palm push

This gesture is very similar to Hitler hands but instead of putting your palm down, you show your palm to the other person; you are unconsciously saying, "Talk to the hand." This is another condescending and rude gesture. It almost looks as though you are ready to shove it into someone's face. Avoid using it, as you will not make any friends if you palm-push them.

The José pose

This pose is reserved for men only. If you are being palm-pushed by an office bully, push back by putting your hands behind your head, leaning back in your chair, and putting your legs in figure four or keeping them slightly open. (Women, you can see why this is not a good pose for you). This is the ultimate, uber-confident, slightly arrogant power pose. I call this the José pose because I worked with a

The José pose.

The gorilla pose.

former Army ranger by that name, and every time the boss would come into his office to chat, he would do that. This is the ultimate confidence pose! He feared no one. Remember this rule: When in doubt, spread out. Taking up space screams importance. Sitting in the José pose with your legs apart assures others that you are large and in charge.

The gorilla pose

The gorilla pose is super effective when you want to deliver information with a punch. I tell salespeople to use this pose when they make their pitch, because people trust those who look confident. To do the gorilla pose, place your hands on a table, and lean over and in toward whoever is sitting nearby. By leaning in you appear to be more personable. If you want to appear even more personable and likeable, smile as you assume the gorilla pose. If you don't, you will still come

across as self-assured, but more aggressive than friendly (see the previous photo of Kelly). Depending on what the situation calls for, you
can either smile or look more stern, as Kelly is here. I call this the
gorilla pose because it resembles a gorilla when it is all puffed up, defending its territory.

Lift your chin

When you see a person walking around with their chin in the
air, that person is seen as having an air of superiority. There is a joke
about Extraverts and Introverts and it goes like this: "How can you
tell if an introvert likes you? He looks at *your* shoes." Think about it:
You have look down your nose at someone when your chin is lifted
in the air. But walking into a room with a wide gait and your chin
lifted will not make you appear to be arrogant; it will make you look
self-assured and confident. I always lift my chin, and when I do I have
better posture and look and feel more powerful.

Don't cover your neck dimple

The neck dimple, or jugular notch, is a very vulnerable part of
the body. When we feel threatened, we unconsciously move to protect this vulnerable area. Our neck allows us to breathe, talk, and
swallow. It also houses two carotid arteries that supply the head and
neck with oxygenated blood, so if our necks were to be attacked, it
could be life-threatening. In the movie *Identity Thief*, the signature
move of Melissa McCarthy's character is to finger strike people's neck
dimples, which then sends them crumpling to the floor. This is a real
martial arts technique. Finger striking the neck dimple can induce
choking and sometimes unconsciousness by crushing the windpipe.

My detainees who came into the interrogation booth scared and
nervous would sit balled up, with their legs tightly pressed together,
their elbows tucked glues to their sides, and one hand covering their
neck. This hand would move to the back of the neck sometimes and
then right back to the neck dimple. They would hold their necks literally for hours. After building rapport—sharing tea and something to

eat, or maybe playing a game—the hand would slowly start to come down. When this happened I knew they were feeling more comfortable and so I would ease into my questions. When an uncomfortable topic came up, so did their hands, right to neck dimple in that protective yet unconscious gesture.

Both women and men cover their neck dimples in stressful situations. Men tend to grab their necks as if they were grabbing their beards and pulling them down, whereas women touch their necks more daintily, sometimes only with the tips of their fingers. In all my observations of colleagues, students, friends, and detainees, I can say that rubbing the neck and covering the neck dimple is an absolute sign of stress. The next time you are playing poker, or inquiring why your boyfriend didn't answer your any of your texts last night, watch for the hands going to the neck. Start to pay attention to exactly *when* they touch their neck during the game or the conversation, because that's the point at which stress is registering, albeit subconsciously.

The neck dimple is also considered to be an erogenous zone. When it's exposed, it says "I'm open" (not to be confused with "I'm easy," fellas). The bottom line about the neck dimple: If you want to appear sure of yourself, confident, and relaxed, do not put your hand anywhere on your neck, or your face for that matter!

So now you know how to position your body to look confident and how, ultimately, these positions and gestures will make you feel confident. Why do you need to be confident? Here's why:

- You will need to start conversations with strangers and still appear confident, powerful, and likeable.
- You will need to be able to control those conversations without getting nervous.
- You will need to build rapport through establishing common ground, flattery, using your body language, changing your personality preferences, and being sincere and empathetic.

- You will need to read other people's body language and baseline them.

- You will need to identify behavioral incongruence through observing deviations in baseline behavior.

- You will need to probe those topics that were being discussed when you observed those deviations with good questioning techniques to uncover the truth.

You need confidence in order to be able to do all of that successfully. The next time you need to confront a bully or stand up for yourself, do the following. First, correct your posture to relax your breathing. Then, widen your stride and walk authoritatively up to the person in question and stand like Superman or Wonder Woman, with 10 inches or so between your feet, raise your chin, and lean in as you address this person, making sure you deepen your voice. Don't forget to smile! You want to be congenial and authoritative at the same time. You will exude confidence, and no bully is going to mess with that. But if you don't feel confident, the bully will see through you and walk all over you. If you need to, you have your steepling techniques and your power poses. If all else fails, use your Hitler hands or the palm push, but only as a last resort!

The confident voice

Even controlling your voice will help you transform how you feel. Speak more loudly and clearly, emphasize key syllables and points, lower the pitch of your voice, "chunk" the information you're conveying, and incorporate pauses so that people have time to digest what you're saying. When the pitch of your voice goes up, and your voice gets softer and more muffled, that is a sure indicator that you're feeling insecure and nervous. Have you ever seen the talk show *Outnumbered* on the Fox News channel? It is comprised of four female newscasters and one male newscaster (hence the name *Outnumbered*) discussing current news events. One of the female panelists is Harris Faulkner. Her voice, above those of all the other female panelists, exudes authority because she speaks in a lower pitch. I *want* to listen to her because she sounds and appears to be more confident than the other female panelists. Plus, I'm more apt to believe what she has to say.

I have spoken to audiences from all different professional backgrounds—health and safety investigators, auditors, arson investigators, pediatric dentists, small-business owners, and entrepreneurs—on body language, detecting deception, and enhanced communication skills. This past year I noted an unfortunate trend. After my speaking engagements, professional women would constantly come up to me and ask me how they should deal with an office bully. It's saddens me to think that women are feeling bullied or threatened at work. To those of you reading this who are in that situation, use what I have outlined in this chapter. You will change the dynamic you have with this person, I promise you!

The next chapter is all about how to build rapport, even with a perfect stranger. I will teach techniques on how to get people to like you, feel comfortable around you, want to be around you, look to you as a leader, listen to you, ask for and take your advice, and respect you. Potential outcomes could include getting a promotion or raise, diffusing an argument between others, winning a case by convincing a jury, having a criminal confess to you, having your family and friends be open and honest with you, and, best of all, surrounding yourself with positive people. Does all of that sound good? Then read on!

6

E Is for Establish Rapport:
Getting People to *Want* to Like You

The question I am asked most often after people find out I interro-gated members of the Taliban and al Qaeda is "What was it like being a woman and talking to those guys?" They all want to know if they disrepected me or if I felt in any way at a disadvantage because of my sex. I tell people it was great because I was almost considered to be a third gender. Yes, I am a woman, but in their eyes I was an American military member who happened to be female. They didn't look at or treat me the same way as they often did the women in their own cul-tures. I had a huge advantage being a "third gender"; in fact, I would bet that any female interrogator would tell you the same thing. Think about it: I was not a big, intimidating male Marine; I was a small, em-pathetic but authoritative female, so the detainees felt more relaxed with me. They didn't have their guards up, as they would with a male interrogator. This is not to say my male counterparts were not as or even more successful than I. Many were, especially those who had similar cultural backgrounds as some of the detainees or spoke their language. (If I could go back and do it again, I would learn Arabic. My college German and Italian languages didn't do my any favors at GTMO, unfortunately. I learned some Arabic while I was there, but if I had known more it would have given me even more common ground with prisoners.)

A funny thing happened one day regarding Arabic. After hours, days, and weeks of interrogating Arabic-speaking detainees, I began to pick up on some key words and phrases. During one interrogation I understood the detainee's answer in Arabic and, without waiting for my interpreter to translate, I launched into another follow-up question. The detainee looked at me in surprise and became angry. He said, "You lie! You speak Arabic!" I had to explain that I didn't, and that just as they were learning English, I was learning their languages. It took a long time for me to regain his trust; lesson learned on my part: Wait for your interpreter to translate!

I was able to gain the detainees' respect through multiple methods. First, I gained it through the respect I was shown by others in authority. My older male interpreter respected me, the male prison guards respected me, and other male military and civilians respected me. People tend to respect those who are respected by others. Having a background in anthropology and archaeology also helped me identify and bridge some of those cultural differences, but even so, I had never stepped foot in the Middle East and I couldn't speak any of the languages (outside of the few words and sayings I learned while I was there). So how was I able to build rapport with my detainees through common ground? I had none, or so I thought.

First I thought about what we did have in common, me and this foreign fighter for al Qaeda who loathes the United States and everything it stands for. *Oh, I know! We're both human beings! If I treat him like a human then hopefully he will reciprocate and treat me like one, too. We are also both in GTMO in a prison; he's detained, and I'm on orders. Oh, and we both have families. I'm not married and I don't have kids, but I have a niece, nephews, and cousins, and I am sure he does, too. We probably both like to eat and drink; maybe I'll find out what he likes to eat and bring it with me to the interrogation as a kind gesture.* I started with the basics. We all breathe the same air, eat, drink, and have emotions, feelings, and beliefs, so if I could establish common ground with any of those things, it's something I could hopefully build on. Even if we didn't not share the same beliefs, I could still empathize with his and show sincerity. Also detainees were usually inquisitive about who I was and how I got there, so that created an opportunity for conversation and hence establishing rapport. You see, you *can* build rapport with anyone, even a terrorist. Some of you may be thinking, *Why would you want to?* Or, *How could you?* The answers are I *had* to, and I could because I knew if I were able to build rapport and gain respect and trust, I would be gaining something far more valuable in the end: intelligence information that would keep the United States and its armed forces and civilians safe. *That's* why and how I was able to do it. Remember: You can build rapport with anyone.

A Day in the Life of an Interrogator

It's late in the evening; the air is still hot, humid, and sticky. My sweat-soaked uniform has since dried out and now I have the chills from the air conditioning blowing overhead in the interrogation booth as I wait with my interpreter for "Ahmed" (name changed for security reasons), my Saudi detainee, to arrive. Enthusiasm was nonexistent; in fact, I was disheartened. Every Saudi detainee I had interrogated up until that point seemed completely hardened and intractable. My Saudi detainees would typically sit across from me, their black eyes glaring at me almost as though they were shooting knives into my soul. I knew that they would have stabbed me if they had the chance, but they were chained and handcuffed to the ground, so that wasn't going to happen. They would scowl and growl at me and say I had the *jinn* (evil genie) in me. I got nowhere with Saudis. I tried every approach and rapport-building technique possible with these guys. That night I was sure I'd be in for another exhausting interrogation that would ultimately end up being another letdown.

I had worked for hours on my interrogation plan; I ran every possible scenario through my head as to how I could get him engaged in conversation. My head was spinning with ideas. Suddenly a door down the hallway opened, with the familiar shout of "Detainee on deck!" interrupting my concentration. My interpreter and I looked at each other and sighed. He knew it was going to be a long night, too. I started having second thoughts. *What if I tried something entirely different? I'll just go with my gut feeling,* I thought. *No plans.* Just then Ahmed appeared at the door flanked by military guards. He was approximately 5 feet 9 inches tall, his hands were clasped together, his shoulders were rolled inward, and his posture was slumped over slightly. As I observed his body language, I knew this was a significant departure from the typical broad-chested, head-held-high, ready-to-fight stance of my other Saudi detainees. His shoulders curling inward told me he was unsure of himself and the situation, possibly nervous or frightened. I smiled. He lifted his head and his eyes caught mine. For a microsecond I saw him leak a tiny smile that flashed on his face before it went right back to a frown. (This is called a *microexpression*, which I will discuss in further detail in Chapter 9.) I knew I was right to go with my gut.

The guards guided him to sit him down in the chair. For the detainees we had metal folding chairs that did not swivel or roll so that the detainees would stay seated securely while chained to the deadbolt in the ground. We interrogators sat in cloth-covered, swiveling, rolling chairs, obviously much more comfortable. As the guards guided him toward the chair, I said, "Stop!" Ahmed looked at me with concern on his face, and so did the guards. I removed his chair and rolled my comfortable chair in front of the deadbolt. "I would like him to sit in this chair," I told the guards. Now my interpreter looked concerned, too. Normally I informed my interpreter of everything I was going to do in the booth so he wouldn't be taken off guard and we could work as a cohesive team. I didn't tell him I was going to swap chairs and have myself sit on the cold, metal chair, because I hadn't planned on it. But my gut told me to do it. My interpreter knew I always did things for a reason and was probably initiating my Plan B. Many times I would initiate Plans E, F, G, too! An interrogator has to be as adaptable as water flowing through crevasses to find its way to the solution.

At first Ahmed resisted, he shook his head back and forth saying, "*Laa!*" which means "no" in Arabic. My interpreter translated: "No, please, I cannot take her chair. Please give me the other chair." I smiled, and, looking straight in his eyes, I said, "Please sit in my chair; I want you to be comfortable tonight." After my interpreter translated, Ahmed gave up resisting and reluctantly sat in the chair. The guards bolted his leg and waist chains to the deadbolt in the floor, and then I instructed them to un-cuff his hands. Ahmed now looked at me and smiled back. I thought to myself, *Is this the right guy?* The guards asked if I needed anything else; I said no and dismissed them. My interpreter and I sat down, bringing our chairs a little closer to Ahmed, into his social space; he didn't seem to mind. There are four types of relationship space zones: intimate, personal, social, and public. These zones differ from country to country. In many countries in the Middle East, these zones tend to be a lot closer, to the point of being virtually nonexistent. For example, people will stand in your intimate space in public, and men will walk hand-in-hand down the streets together as a sign of respect. But for Americans, the zones are more clearly delineated. Intimate space is typically a 1.5 foot buffer zone around you into which you allow only a spouse/significant other and children. Personal space is approximately a 1.5-foot to 4-foot buffer zone, where you let in only close friends and family. Social space is approximately a 4-foot to 12-foot buffer zone into which you let in acquaintances and coworkers. And public space is anything outside of a 12-foot buffer zone, where the rest of the world exists.

As the saying goes, when in Rome, do what the Romans do. As my interpreter and I leaned in together and were about to engage my detainee in conversation, he started speaking immediately in Arabic. I listened while my interpreter translated: "Thank you so much for the nice chair. I feel badly for taking it, but thank you." I checked my file, asked him his name and some other questions, and confirmed that in fact I had the right detainee. Fast-forward three months later and Ahmed and I established incredible rapport, which led to a relationship of mutual respect, all created purposefully on my part, of course. We shared tea together and exchanged stories and even some laughter, and I gave him special privileges for his cooperation. He gave more information to me during those three months than I ever could have imagined.

One day he asked me to sneak him into interrogation later that night because he had something secret to tell me. He didn't want the others seeing him for fear they would think he was cooperating with us (which he was) and retaliate against him. His information ended up being so valuable that it launched a huge investigation inside the camp. He became sought after by other entities because of the cooperation and level of trust and rapport I had built with him. A few days later, after terminating one of our interrogations, I was standing in the doorway waiting for the guards to bring him back to his cell, and he asked me, "Do you want to know why I cooperated with you and told you all of that information over the past few months?" I smiled and said, "Yes, Ahmed, I do." He replied, "Because you were so nice to me that first day, giving me the comfortable chair, that I had to be nice to you. You respected me and so I had to respect you. It's my culture." Had I not listened to my gut feeling, I never would have been able to build that relationship with Ahmed, and, certainly, I never would have gotten the intelligence information I did. All because of a comfortable chair.

Generally speaking, people feel the need to reciprocate acts of kindness, whether it's a simple smile or helping someone—even detainees in GTMO. This is a common elicitation technique called *quid pro quo*, Latin for "this for that." Usually if you share something personal with someone he will share something personal with you; if you offer to buy someone a drink, he will buy one for you in return. You get the idea. It's simple, and it works.

Getting Anyone to Like You

Wouldn't you want to know how to get people to *want* to like you? Of course you would! I will tell you how to accomplish that with 10 specific rapport-building techniques. If you understand that people like people who are similar to them, then this chapter will be your bread and butter for creating long-lasting, meaningful personal and professional relationships that can then lead to increased trust (from a significant other) or even an increase in income (from your boss). After all, it's not the product that makes a sale; it's the salesperson who makes the sale through the relationship she builds with the buyer by using rapport and persuasion. I train salespeople and small-business owners on rapport-building skills and enhanced communication skills to make them better at what they do. People do not want to buy things they need from people they don't like, but people will almost always buy from people they like, even things they don't need!

Rapport is a feeling, the connection created between two or more people when they are interacting and communicating with each other. It is also behavior, the things people do that help them relate to one another. Rapport is about empathy, respect, trust, acceptance, and sincerity. It's about connecting on an emotional level. You can show another person that you can identify with her by listening with sincerity, understanding how she views the world, and respecting her views, whatever they may be. This is especially important when interacting with people from other cultures and showing respect for their cultural norms. Ultimately, rapport is a mutual, positive relationship, and when you have it, you have a bond and, thus, a relationship.

You may have read that there is such a thing as both positive and negative rapport-building, and I agree with this. The difference between the two is this: When you build positive rapport with someone, you do so by getting someone to like you by saying or doing things that encourage that person's respect, admiration, interest, and sincerity. When you build negative rapport, you do it by doing things that could be considered immoral or unethical, such as bribing someone with special incentives or perks, or building common ground at the expense of others (usually by ridiculing others or engaging in condescending or hurtful banter). My advice? Don't engage in negative rapport-building; it can end up being costly in the end, not to mention the fact that it's just not nice.

Some authors who have written on this subject contend that rapport is not necessarily about getting someone to like you. I disagree with this. You can't have a positive relationship with someone you don't like. Rapport can certainly be used to get people to like you, because remember: People like other people who are similar to them. How do you become similar to other people? By finding or creating common ground with them. Common ground may be that you both like the same football team, or you are both from the same city, or you both have dogs, or you both enjoy sailing. You get the idea. You can build common ground on the largest of topics, too; you both have families, or you both enjoy the art of negotiation. Whatever that common ground is, find it with the person with whom you are trying to build rapport, whether you're giving a sales pitch, interrogating a prisoner, arresting a criminal, negotiating a divorce settlement, or doing your best to ace a job interview. Establishing common ground is just one rapport technique. I am going to give you 10 more you can use to get people to like you, to want to converse with you, and to admire and trust you. My 10 rapport-building techniques are as follows:

1. Smile.
2. Use touch, carefully.
3. Share something about yourself (*quid pro quo*).
4. Mirror or match, cautiously.
5. Demonstrate respect.
6. Use open body language.
7. Suspend your ego.
8. Flatter and praise.
9. Take your time and listen.
10. Get the person moving and talking.

Let's discuss each one in further detail.

1. Smile.

There are two types of smiles: a sincere smile and a sales smile. In a sincere smile, a person smiles with his eyes; you can see crow's feet, or smile lines, around the eyes. In a fake or sales smile, there are no corresponding smile lines around the eyes. I flash a sales smile for photos purposely so my crow's feet don't show! To accompany a sincere smile, try also raising your eyebrows. Raised eyebrows indicate interest. This subconsciously tells the other person you are interested in him or that he should be interested in what you just said. When we look at babies and cute cuddly animals, we are usually wide-eyed and smiling. Why? Seeing how adorable they are generally elates us, and we want them to see us the same way. Dolls and cartoon princesses all have huge eyes so that they are visually pleasing. Therefore, the bigger our eyes are (within reason, of course), the more attractive we are to others. Interestingly, our pupils will also dilate when we see something interesting or attractive. The eyes express so much without words; use yours to your advantage.

So, in order to appear sincere when your boss shows you pictures of her newborn baby (which you really think looks like a constipated, red pickle), offer a sincere smile (remember to crinkle your eyes) and raise your eyebrows as you say, "How adorable!" Smile when you're on the phone, too. Did you know that you can actually hear someone smiling? Of course it's a little harder to tell if the smile is sincere, but you can listen for sincerity. You can also hear whether someone has energy and enthusiasm. Smiling will give you charisma. People who smile come across as optimistic; the more confidence you have, the more energy you have; conversely, the less confidence you have, the less energy and charisma you have. People like other people who are positive, upbeat, happy, and optimistic—in a word, charismatic. We tend to trust people with these qualities more than we do people who appear quiet, shy, unhappy, lackadaisical, or boring. It never hurts to smile!

2. Use touch, carefully

When trying to make a good first impression, you need a strong, unforgettable introduction. You want people to remember you by getting them feel good about themselves. The first time we touch people when we meet them is typically through a handshake. Depending on where in the world you are, follow the cultural norms for greeting a stranger (in some countries this could be a bow). In the United States, we like a firm handshake; other countries prefer a softer, gentler handshake. Don't overdo it by squeezing so tightly you cut off circulation, or shaking so enthusiastically you give the other person a headache. A slightly firm grip while shaking up and down once or twice will suffice. People ask me what a proper handshake is. A proper handshake is always a reciprocal handshake. Always match your handshake to the other person's. Also, make sure you don't have sweaty palms. Wipe those mitts dry first, either in your pocket, behind your back, or on the front of your suit jacket, as though you were straightening it. Also, never use the politician's handshake, the two hands handshake, unless you are shaking hands with an elderly person or want to express sincere sympathy. You should never use the politician handshake for control; it's an instant rapport killer.

After the handshake, the initial touch, there is the follow-up touch. I know this sounds a bit strange, even provocative, but I assure you it is not. In today's society, touch seems to be restricted only to those people we know really well, such as family and friends. How your family handled touch when you were growing up, whether you hugged a lot or never showed affection, will have an effect on how you feel about touching others now. Also, with the ever-present spectre of sexual-harassment charges hanging over everything, people tend to err on the side of keeping their hands to themselves. I don't blame them. But what we may be missing is the important message that touch brings. Touching a stranger respectfully and professionally can bring about a deeper sense of connection and bonding and help you build rapport. Sometimes touch can speak for us when words fail; a hand on the shoulder when someone just told you he had to put his dog down says, "I'm so sorry, I am here for you." Touching doesn't just involve other people, of course. We also do what I refer to as self-preening—twirling our hair, keeping our arms close to our sides, hugging ourselves, picking at our cuticles, rubbing our upper lip with one finger, massaging the stress out of our neck, or rubbing our hands up and down our arms. All of these gestures send a soothing, calming message to our brain. How the brain responds to the touch of others depends on the context: who is touching you and in what type of setting.

Using touch when you first meet someone means you will be touching a stranger, so you should know the safe zones. The upper back and the shoulder down to the elbow are typically the safe zones where both genders can touch one another safely. It is never okay to touch the lower back. This is an intimate zone. If you see two of your colleagues together and a male escorts a female through a door while his hand gently touches her lower back, he's either a real boundary-buster or they are sleeping together. Abiding by the rules of safe zones, try to incorporate touch with someone new at least three times within the first 10–15 minutes of the conversation. Your first touch is the opening handshake. Your second could be a light touch on the back of the shoulder as you introduce Jane to Bob. The third could be a gentle tap on the upper arm, accompanied by a shared joke or laugh. The fourth could be shaking the person's hand one more time before you depart, as you tell the person how much you enjoyed meeting him. You just touched a stranger, safely, four times.

3. Share something about yourself.

People tend to want to reciprocate confidences and positive behavior, so share something personal about yourself by using the *quid pro quo* elicitation technique I discussed earlier. For instance, if I confided to you that I was pulled over for speeding last night and got a ticket for $180, I would expect you to come back and share a similar experience. If you responded by saying, "That stinks. I got pulled over last week but was able to get out of the ticket because it was my birthday," I would know you are comfortable sharing personal information with me. I could then choose to share more secret or sensitive information in hopes that you would reciprocate in kind.

I am often hired as a role player to test students during their training. In one test my goal is to get them to share sensitive information with me. I do this by using the *quid pro quo* technique. I don't share real sensitive information with them; I make it up. Their information, however, is legitimate. If I can get them to think that I trust them enough to open up and confide in them, they usually dive in and share their own secrets with me. Essentially I am exploiting the fact that people are generally trusting of trusting people, but because it's training, I have to do it in this particular circumstance.

Using *quid pro quo* can help you uncover common ground. Going back to the previous example, let's say you shared with me that you were pulled over, too, so maybe our common ground is that we both like to drive fast, or we both think the speed limit should be raised, or we both believe that cops have nothing better to do than to hand out tickets. Of course, you can find common ground with people without even trying. I usually like to sleep on a plane. However, if I hear my neighbor speaking in the same accent as mine (which is rare, because not many people "speak" Rhode Island), I instantly feel we have a connection or share a commonality, so I am more likely to strike up a conversation with that person. I have seen strangers pass each other while walking on the speed walkways in airports and giving each other high-fives in the air or nods of approval because they are both wearing the same sports team jersey. Similarly, my dad is a Harley guy, and when we go out riding together, anyone we pass who is also on a motorcycle, even if it's not a Harley-Davidson, waves because we are part of the same club that likes motorcycles. See how easy it is to find common ground? Once you both say "Me too!" or "I totally agree with you!" you are connected emotionally through rapport. Let the negotiating or pitching begin!

Here's another example. You're in long line of people at the grocery store, waiting to check out, and you can see the cashier is frustrated and taking it out on customers. By the time you get up to her, she's in an even worse mood than she was before. You haven't done anything but patiently wait in that line, so why should you be treated with disrespect just because she's having a bad day? You shouldn't. So next time, change her attitude by using this technique. Trust me, it works! I used it myself once when I was in a line that extended halfway down an aisle, it was so long. I could see the cashier was already frustrated about trying to check people out as fast as she could, and I knew that when she saw my basket of stuff, it would only increase her agitation. One by one, all the customers in front of me started mirroring her attitude. When it was my turn, I decided to change her attitude instead. I walked up to her, gave her a big smile, put my basket on the counter, and said, "And to think I came in for two things. Ugh!" She paused, looked up at me, relaxed her shoulders, smiled, and said with a sigh, "You are just like me! I do that all the time." I built common ground with her, but it was my smile that really broke through her unhappy disposition. I don't think any other person in that line smiled at her. *Quid pro quo*, people! You get back what you give.

4. Mirror or match, cautiously.

Rapport can be established by mirroring a person's body language, vocal tone and pitch, words and phrases, rate and speed of blinking, and even breathing. Mirroring body language (*isopraxism*, if you want the fancy term) involves displaying the same posture and movements as the person you are with, but in a mirror image. In the following image, Kelly (right) is holding a wine glass in his left hand, while Chris (left) is holding his glass in his right hand. They are a perfect mirror image of each other. Let's say you are at a job interview, and the interviewer is sitting behind a desk. At one point she leans in and rests her left elbow on the desk, with her hand under her chin. If you wanted to mirror her, you would cross your left leg over your right knee, lean in, rest your right elbow on the top of your knee, and touch your fingers to your chin.

Mirroring.

Matching body language is the inverse of mirroring; it occurs when you display the exact same body posture, but without the mirror image. In the following image, Kelly and Chris are matching each other by holding their wine glass in their right hand. Going back to the previous example, if the interviewer were resting her chin on her right hand, you would rest your chin on your right hand, and so on.

Both mirroring and matching require the conscious study of another person's behavior, but they need to occur outside the conscious awareness of the other person so that they appear natural and unconscious on your part. It's important you don't mimic the other person, as that will only destroy rapport. To this end, avoid making sudden

Matching.

movements, and wait 30 seconds until you start matching/mirroring the other person's movements or speech. As well, put your own spin on your responses and vary them so that they are slightly different from the other person's. The second someone catches on to what you are doing is the second you look like an idiot. If you've ever caught someone copying you, it was probably annoying and a little creepy, right? But if you can *subtly* match your movements and speech to those of others, subconsciously they will think you are similar to them and, thus, feel they can build a connection more easily. It's almost as though you were creating common ground simply by looking and sounding like the other person.

When the other person starts to mirror or match you uncon-sciously in return, this is called pacing and leading. Try it out today at work or tonight at home. See if you can get your coworker or family member to start mirroring or matching your posture and gestures. When he or she does, he or she is fully in tune with you and probably hanging on your every word. You can mirror and match people over the phone, too—just use the same words, speech patterns, vocabu-lary, tone, pitch, and volume. If you talk and sound like them, they will like you without even knowing it and—*voilà!*—you have rapport. I often use this technique when I have to call the technology help desk. Because I am technologically challenged, I know I am going to frustrate the person on the other end of the line, so I start building rapport as soon as I can. I can usually hear the other person smiling over the phone by the time we hang up.

If you ever have to work with an interpreter, match and mirror the person you are talking to, even though you cannot understand each other's language. Do not let the interpreter do the matching or mirroring because then your interpreter will be the one building rap-port! Good interrogators train their interpreters to match or mirror their body language so that they work and act as one. Even though the detainee only understands the interpreter, rapport is (hopefully) established with the interrogator since the interrogator is the one set-ting the pace.

I often find that mirroring verbally is easier and more effective than mirroring the body. If I mirror someone's tone and pitch of voice, and rate and pattern of speech, versus mirroring posture and gestures, I sound like that person, and hence they think I am similar to them. For instance, Introverts tend to speak softly and slowly and think about what to say and how to say it for fear of putting their foot in their mouth. As an Extravert, I tend to speak loudly and quickly, and quite often I put my foot in my mouth. So when I converse with more introverted people I have to tone it down so I am more like them. (I will speak more on personality preferences in Chapter 7.)

An example of how I use words to mirror is my blond witch story. I was grocery shopping one day and wandered up to the wine tasting table. The gentleman behind the table handed me a tasting cup and just before I could take it, he pulled it back. "Do you have ID?" he demanded in a condescending voice. I thought, *Wow, what a compliment!* I handed him my license that had a picture of me circa 2002 with dark hair, the color I was born with. "You had dark hair," he sneered. *Nothing like stating the obvious*, I thought. Not happy with his attitude, I decided to use my rapport-building skills to get him to act a bit friendlier toward me. "Yeah, I use this thing called bleach," I replied with a big smile.

He handed my license back to me and began pouring the wine. "I call it witchcraft," he said.

"Well, witchcraft costs a lot of money," I jokingly replied.

He looked up and smiled. Success! At that point another female shopper with blond hair joined our conversation. "I use witchcraft, too, and it's draining my wallet," she said as she leaned in and pretended to whisper confidentially to me. Both of us used his word (witchcraft) and it made him feel good. Soon the three of us were chatting away as we tasted the wine. I bought a bottle and left happy. There is power in using other people's words. People will pick up on the fact that you are doing it, and it makes them feel that you are paying attention to them. And let's face it: who doesn't want attention?

5. Demonstrate respect.

What comes around goes around. Karma is a bitch. What you dish out, you get back. All of these sayings basically say that how we treat others is how we'll be treated in return. If you aren't going to give it, you aren't going to get it; it's that simple. So how do you show respect so you can get respect? First, allow people to have their own views and opinions, just as you would want others to allow you to have yours. Sometimes you have to agree to disagree, which requires ego suspension. Be courteous, polite, professional, and non-confrontational. Show esteem, admiration, and honor toward each and every person. As I would always tell my students who were training to be interrogators, you attract more bees with honey than with vinegar. In other words, you'll get more from people if you are nice. Who wants to give anything, whether it's a discount, a freebee, advice, or sensitive information, to a mean person?

I tried to instill in new interrogators that no matter what heinous crime a detainee committed—and believe me, many were beyond heinous—they were still human beings and should be treated as such. The inexperienced interrogators I worked with always reverted to saying something along the lines of "Tell me the truth, or else!" Or else what? Or else they stay in prison? Or they won't get a cigarette? Detainees would refuse to cooperate if they heard that. They became defensive, confrontational, and even aggressive. It only makes sense. It's like a parent yelling at a child, "Clean your room, or else!" That approach isn't typically effective because it just makes the child defiant. These detainees didn't care because they knew we couldn't and wouldn't make them talk. The only choice we had was to get them to *want* to talk. We didn't have to ask "pretty please," but we did need to show some respect while still being the authority figure. When I showed my detainees respect, most of them respected me in return, and that is how I built rapport and obtained intelligence information. So the next time you are in a restaurant and the waitress brings you the wrong order, instead of griping at her and calling her incompetent, try politely saying, "I'm so sorry, but this is the wrong order. Would you mind bringing me what I ordered so I can eat with my family? Thank you so much." She'll probably hustle to go find your order instead of spit in your food.

The other advantage to being respected is that you also gain trust. When you get someone to trust you, you will be allowed into his or her personal space. We let our guards down with people we trust and tell them our fears, desires, and secrets.

6. Use open body language.

If you want people to open up to you, you first have to open your body language. If you close up your body language, people will close themselves off to you. To keep your body language open, expose the three vulnerable zones that I mentioned earlier: the neck dimple, the belly, and the groin area. When all three vulnerable zones are open and exposed, you are unconsciously saying, *I trust you not to hurt me; I trust that you won't hit me in the neck dimple and collapse my trachea, or punch me in the belly, or kick me in the groin.* By the way, if you have never been hit in the stomach, be thankful. I used to practice Shorin Ryu Karate more than a decade ago. I was a brown belt and in the best shape of my life. In one drill I was up against a 16-year-old black belt named Manni who was a powerful fighter. I had to block his punches, but needless to say I didn't block the first one; he hit me in the stomach and knocked the wind out of me. It was the first time I had ever gotten the wind knocked out of me and I thought I was going to die. I literally could not breathe. When my breath finally came back, Manni said, "Now you'll block my punch," and I sure did! Speaking from experience, the stomach is a very vulnerable zone. Exposing this and the other vulnerable spots tells people you are confident and open to them. It silently broadcasts that you trust them, and hopefully they will trust you, too.

Try not to cross your arms in front of your chest. People almost always take this gesture as defensive or rejecting, and most of the time it is. Not always; sometimes people will do this when they are thinking or just cold. But most people will see it as defensive, so don't do it). Also, keep your palms open and exposed; don't face your palms inward toward your body or, worse, hide your hands by stuffing them in your pockets. Finally, don't close yourself off by putting up barriers between you and the other person. A barrier can be a desk, a computer screen, a pile of papers, or even a glass of wine. Your body can be used as a barrier, too. For instance, if a man approaches a woman seated at a bar and she has no interest in him, she will look over her shoulder, with her arm remaining between them, to politely refuse his advance.

Her arm and shoulder are her barriers. She may even prop up her purse for reinforcement.

Remove all barriers between you and the person with whom you are trying to build rapport, because a barrier will block communication. When I was interrogating detainees, I would usually keep the table off to the side so I could take notes; or, I would just take notes with my notepad on my lap. I removed all barriers that I could between the detainees and myself. I wanted to open myself up as much as possible to win their trust and, ultimately, form an emotional bond with them, which would then elicit shame if they were to lie to me.

7. Suspend your ego.

Sometimes you have to be open to advice, education, and criticism in order to build rapport. People who have inflated egos have a hard time being corrected, criticized (not degrading criticism, but constructive criticism), taught, or advised. So for example, you will need to learn to suspend your ego and your pride when a potential new client wants to teach you the importance of branding for her company, even though you are a marketing director. I had to do this many, many times, and I still do it to this day, because I have a security clearance and can't talk about what I do anyway. The upside is that I let people feel good about educating me. People with security clearances can't disclose details about their jobs, especially to people who don't have a security clearance. If a bunch of people without clearances are trying to one-up each other by sharing stories about the projects they are working on, people with clearances can't join in and share anything about what they are working on. Navy Special Forces are in the same boat; when they are around other sailors, even in the intelligence community, they can't share any information about what they do, where they have deployed, or what missions they've gone on. This used to be especially hard for me when I heard people talk about all the torture and abuse that allegedly happened in GTMO. I was there, and I didn't witness any type of torture or abuse (physical or mental) of detainees, but unfortunately I had to bite my tongue while they vented their ignorance, because they didn't have a "need to know."

8. Flatter and praise.

Flattery, when done artfully, makes people feel good. When people feel good they want to share more about themselves to make you realize just how great they really are. Just don't overdo it. If you lay the flattery on thick, people will see right through you, and you will lose all credibility and rapport. You can flatter people on their physical appearance if it's socially acceptable. If a coworker loses 30 pounds, for example, it's okay to say, "You look great and you must feel so healthy." When flattering the opposite sex, however, it's always safer to flatter about nonphysical attributes such as the other person's work ethic, dedication, assistance in a new project, role as a mentor, subject-matter expertise, and so on. If you're a man, avoid saying to a woman, "Wow, you look great in that dress." I would flatter my detainees by telling them I knew how proud they were of their culture, religion, and family, or that the other detainees looked up to them as role models. The trick to flattering or giving praise is being genuine and sincere; the rule is that a little goes a long way.

9. Take your time and listen.

Nodding your head up and down in the affirmative tells someone, "Keep talking. I'm listening and I'm interested." It also says "I agree with you," "I like what you are saying," or "I want to hear more." Add an eyebrow raise and it augments the message of interest. If you see someone nod at you like this as she flashes a sales smile, be leery—she's probably just appeasing you as she's figuring out a way to escape the conversation. Be sure to listen to people. Don't cut them off, jump the gun and answer a question before they are finished asking it, or finish their sentences for them. All of these habits are annoying and send the signal that you would rather hear yourself talk. When you show people you are interested in what they have to say, they will appreciate it, and it will make them feel important. Learn to slow down and take the time to really hear what they are saying. If you aren't listening, you'll miss critical information.

During my interrogations, I would get so anxious to ask the next question that I would often forget to pause to see whether the detainee would freely add more information without my having to ask a follow-up question. Pausing is actually a great technique because it creates silence. Most people find silence awkward and uncomfortable, so they will quickly pick up the conversation again just to alleviate the awkwardness. I tell people to enjoy the silence. If you create a space for silence and let others do most of the talking, two things happen: First, they will give you information; second, their ego will get a boost, because it exploits the fact that people love to be heard and hear themselves talk. This makes them feel good, and you know what happens when we make people feel good: They are more apt to like us. Because my job was to get information, I often sat back and let the detainees carry the conversation; after all, when I was talking, they weren't.

10. Get them talking and moving.

This is the last rapport-building technique because by this point in the conversation, you should have already established some rapport; now you just want to strengthen it. We already know that letting people talk is a good thing. Now you really want to get them to warm up to you to stay engaged in the conversation. You do that by asking open-ended questions that require a narrative response, versus yes-or-no questions. Another good way to do this is to ask for help. For example, say you are on a plane and you ask a stranger to help you open the overhead compartment to put your bag in; or you are in a crowded bar, and instead of squeezing between patrons to order a drink, you ask a person sitting at the bar to order one for you. When you ask people for a favor, and they do it, they end up feeling good about themselves for helping. I used to work with a retired FBI agent who was a behavioral analysis expert. He would often say that no one helps others just to be kind; they do it to make themselves feel good. I don't disagree with this in theory, but are we really that selfish? I think there is definitely an element of wanting to feel good in any act of altruism. Jody Arias did this with reporters while in jail. She proved to be very cunning and often used her looks to deceive people. She knew the trick of getting people to do something for her so that she could build rapport. While in jail preparing to be interviewed by reporters in 2008, she engaged reporters in non-pertinent, friendly chit-chat, and then asked them to bring her a compact so she could "freshen up her makeup." She even said, "Don't roll the cameras yet." Jodi was trying to get everyone on her side and to think of her as the pretty, innocent victim. Remember: To sell yourself, a product, or an idea, the first step is to get people to talk to you.

Asking for favors and asking open-ended questions will help keep your target engaged. Now let's get him moving. If you have the opportunity, move around as you are talking to someone. It can give the impression that you have spent hours together in many different locales when in reality, you have only spent a few minutes in each other's presence. Walking and moving around will also relieve stress. If you are an attorney who is about to interview a new witness, try to start the conversation as soon as you meet him in the lobby; then continue to talk with him as you make your way to the actual meeting place. If you take a break, have both of you walk to the coffee shop or concession stand and back to the meeting area. When you close the meeting, walk the witness out. The witness will feel as though he has spent an entire day with you and feel more closely connected to you.

All in the Family

It is really difficult for me to use my skills on my friends and family, but sometimes I have to. When my colleague Serge and I were forming our company, he actually came up with the name and symbol (and I'm usually the artsy, creative one). I loved it instantly. I developed our brochure with the new name and logo and sent a copy to my brother, who designed our Website. He printed out our brochure and walked it over to my parents. I got a phone call from my mom as I was battling Virginia Beach rush hour traffic: "Dad wants to talk to you." *Oh god, here it comes*, I thought, because my dad made her call me for a reason.

"Leen?"

"Yeah, Dad."

"I don't understand this congruency name. [My company's name is The Congriency Group.] I don't like it. What does it mean? You know a name of company is everything. Steve Jobs had a hard time getting Apple to take off because of its name. The average Joe isn't going to know what congruency means. I don't know...you'd better re-think it."

As I tried to explain the meaning of the name and why we choose it, I felt myself slipping back to my typical way of conversing with my dad: on the defensive! I am just like him (stubborn). When we get something in our heads, it is going to take moving the moon to convince us otherwise. As the conversation went on I realized I was arguing with him. I thought, *What do I do for a living? I teach people how to diffuse arguments! Why can't I do this with my dad?* So I flipped on the switch and started using my techniques, using word repetition (I will talk about how to repeat words to diffuse an argument in a moment), asking him to offer an explanation (because I certainly wasn't changing the name!), and flattery. I asked him what he thought I should do, and he responded that I had to explain the name somehow. I responded by suggesting we put the history of the company's name on the brochure and Website. Ultimately we agreed. I left that conversation making him feel good for *his* suggestion. In hindsight, it was a good suggestion, and you will see the explanation of my company's name on both our Website and brochure. But the reason I told you that story was to prove that I had to swallow my ego and listen to his constructive criticism, as well as be patient and listen attentively in order to have a mutually respectful conversation. I changed the fate of that conversation for the better. When you realize you have fallen into the trap of arguing with someone or getting frustrated trying to prove a point or explain something, stop and take a breath, and employ your new rapport-building techniques! Suspend your ego, use flattery, be respectful, mirror/march that person, listen attentively, repeat words that other person uses, and smile. Here is another example of these techniques in action:

Son: "It's not fair that you took my PlayStation away!"

Mom: "So you don't think it's fair that I took your PlayStation away?"

Son: "Yeah! My friend's mom never takes his stuff away!"

Mom: "Your friend's mom never takes his stuff away, huh?"

Son: "No! You are not fair!"

Mom: "So, to clarify, I'm not being fair to you by taking away your PlayStation because you don't do your homework. Am I right?"

Son: "I do my homework, Mom!"

Mom: "Hmm, you do your homework, but I got a note from the school saying you haven't."

Son: "I *did* do it; I just forgot to turn it in."

Mom: "So because you forgot to turn it in, I am unfair. Is that right?"

Son: "Okay, okay, I'll make sure to turn it in tomorrow."

Mom: "Good! Turn in your homework on time and I'll be fair with you."

So instead of the son storming off to his room, slamming the door, and ignoring her for the rest of the evening, the mom calmed him down through the art of conversation and word repetition. Trust me, it is as easy as this, and I use it all the time with family and colleagues. (I realize, of course, that if they read this book, my secret is out!)

Mirroring, which I've already discussed, is another great technique to use when trying to diffuse an argument. If you incorporate pauses and slow your rate of speech when you're engaged in a heated discussion, you are not backing down; in fact, you are gaining the upper hand. Because people who speak more slowly and with a lower-pitched voice seem more confident and calm, the aggressor will soon feel foolish raising his voice or getting emotional. Your goal is to get the aggressor to pace and lead you, especially your demeanor, in order to calm everyone down and have a rational conversation.

Five Tips for Enhanced Communication Skills

Building rapport will enhance your interpersonal communication skills, I promise you. But I want to share some other tools that will help you communicate effectively and build respectful, reciprocal relationships, both personal and professional. Here are five tips to add to your arsenal of enhanced communication skills.

1. Manage your emotions.

If you take things personally, you will be emotional and irrational. Realize that sometimes you are talking to the role/title/position, not the person. And the position, not the person filling it, may tell you that you are not meeting expectations. You can't dislike someone or get mad at someone who is doing her job, even if she could use a little more finesse doing it. Try not to feel personally attacked when people offer you constructive criticism or advice on how you could do things better. Likewise, if you can't handle the truth, don't ask for advice. Don't be offended when people stand up for what they believe and it's the opposite of what you believe. We are all entitled to our opinions. And don't take it personally when someone disagrees with you. Never feel that you have to defend yourself; just provide the facts with a calm demeanor (as I am still learning to do with my dad).

2. Agree to disagree.

If you expect people to always like you or agree with you, you are setting yourself up for disappointment. You have to accept that you cannot change people. The idea that we can change others is a major cause in relationship struggles. If one half of the partnership thinks that, over time, he or she can change their partner, let me just be blunt with you and say: *Give it up, it's not going to happen.* We are all guilty of this to some degree. I was in a relationship with a great guy but he was an introvert and I kept expecting him to change to meet my extraversion preferences; of course, it didn't happen. I wanted it to work because he was trustworthy and honest, but I realized I couldn't, and shouldn't, want to change him, and ultimately, the relationship ended. So if you think, *I'll get him to like wine and the theater eventually,* or *She'll learn to love to cook,* or *He'll become more open with his feelings and communicate better,* or *She'll have more ambition after she realizes her potential,* you're in for a huge disappointment. Don't expect people to like you, either, even though admittedly it can be a huge blow to our ego when we realize we aren't liked. And finally, don't expect people to agree with you all the time. Sometimes you will just have to agree to disagree and move on. If done with mutual respect, you may be pleasantly surprised that the other person respects you for standing by your beliefs, and may come around and see it your way. I have noticed that when I am engaged in a conversation with another person and we both agree to disagree, what we were disagreeing about in the first place assumes less importance in the greater scheme of things. The next time you find yourself trying to tell people what or how to think, say this instead: "Wouldn't you agree?" If they don't, that's okay.

3. Be aware.

Inattentional blindness, assumptions, and biases can negatively affect your rapport with others. The term *inattentional blindness* means that we don't see what we don't expect to see. It can also mean we don't hear what we don't expect to hear, and we don't experience what we don't expect to experience. Some of you have probably seen that awareness test video on YouTube with the dancing gorilla or moonwalking bear walking through a crowd of people passing a ball. In the video, half of the people are dressed in white clothes the other half in black clothes. The video asks you to count how many times the team in white passes a ball. But while you are busy counting, a dancing gorilla or moonwalking bear walks right through the middle of the people throwing a ball around. When I play this test for people, very few see the gorilla or bear. Why? Once I replay it, they see the animal as clear as day and are usually shocked they didn't see it the first time around. The reason is because they didn't expect to see a gorilla or a bear; they were too busy counting how many times the team in white passed the ball. Why is overcoming inattentional blindness is so important? Let me give you an example of how intattentional blindness almost cost me an interrogation, and another example of how an assumption made me look stupid (and made me really mad at myself in the process!).

My first story takes place in an interrogation booth. I was interrogating a detainee, and although he wasn't confrontational, he wasn't friendly, either. I had not broken through to him, so we had no rapport. I was trying to engage him in conversation and make eye contact, but he would look at the floor while he gave vague, one-or-two-word answers. He was completely tuning me out and I was getting frustrated. I knew I couldn't force him to talk to me or like me. At that point my interpreter turned to me and whispered in my ear, "You know he's praying, right? That's why he's tuning you out." I didn't know he was praying. I looked over at him and he was lightly tapping his fingertips together mimicking the motion of counting prayer beads. A-ha! I didn't expect to see him praying so I didn't see him praying. My inattentional blindness made me so focused on trying to build rapport and gain eye contact I never saw what his hands were doing. So I gently leaned over and put my hand on his hands and asked very politely if he could stop praying while we talked and told him I would give him time to pray at the end of the interrogation, alone in the room. There is a cultural reason as to why I touched him. As a female I was considered "unclean," and he could only pray if he was clean. So I knew that by touching him, he couldn't go back to praying. I could have lost rapport with him, but it was worth the risk. He did get upset with me initially, but I was able to regain his trust, especially when I let him pray alone properly at the end of the interrogation, as I said I would. Had my interpreter not told me he was praying, my inattentional blindness might have caused me to end that interrogation prematurely out of frustration and not collect any information that day.

My second story has to do with reading body language. The husband of a friend used to study NLP. Knowing what I do, he told me one day, "I want to do an exercise with you. I am going to say three things. One will be a lie. Tell me what the lie is." I thought, *Oh, fun!* He said, "I speak Icelandic, I studied jujitsu, and when I was 11 I won the state national chess championship." Right away my gut instinctively told me that he was lying about the chess, because not only did he give more details about that than the other two statements, but he also rose up on his toes, leaned in to me, and shrugged his shoulders as he said it. Four clusters of deceptive tells right there! Then I said, "You don't speak Icelandic." Why? Because I assumed there was no way he could have. See how an assumption can affect your thinking? I knew he lied about playing chess, but because I let my assumption get the best of me, I missed the real lie. I was so mad at myself. I usually don't assume anything, a golden rule when you are an interrogator, but that day, I fell victim to it. Shame on me!

4. Favorably influence people.

We want to influence people in a positive way. We want them to like us, trust us, respect us, and feel comfortable around us. Here are three ways you can favorably influence others, what I call the three Es:

- **Energize:** Have a positive, upbeat attitude. People want to be around those who are positive; no one wants to be around a Debbie downer or an energy zapper. Positive energy is infectious. I was once told I have an infectious smile; it was the nicest compliment because it meant that I could to make others smile.

- **Encourage:** Be sincere and empathic toward others to encourage them open up and share their feelings, thoughts, and ideas. The best leaders are those who make their subordinates feel that they can voice their concerns and views without any repercussions. People look to other people for confirmation, and trust people with authority. To be regarded as someone with authority, strive to be a respected leader.

- **Engage:** Don't rush rapport or conversation. Responding too quickly in a conversation says that you weren't listening to what the other person just said; you were thinking about what you were going to say. Even if you heard that person, it sends the signal you didn't listen. It also gives the impression to others that what you have to share has more importance. Engaging is always a two-way street.

5. Don't be afraid to let them teach you.

This last tip requires ego suspension and works great on people with big egos. There are two elicitation techniques that you can use to get people to teach you: One is by pretending to be naïve (I call it playing stupid), and the other is expressing disbelief (even if fabricated). For example, when I was interrogating I would play stupid to the fact that I didn't know certain things about my detainees, such as whom they were affiliated with, where they got their training, who they knew in the prison, and so on. I used this technique to get information, and it worked, especially on those detainees with big egos, because they liked feeling that they were smarter than I was or knew more than I did. I put them in a position where they felt I had no clue and that they could do me a favor by teaching me. You can bet I was a good student!

Likewise, when you express disbelief—"I can't *believe* you increased your sales that much in just six months"—people will tend to want to explain how awesome they are and how they did it. Both of these techniques allow the other person to get up on their soapbox and be heard.

You now have 10 rapport-building techniques and five tips you can use to enhance your interpersonal communication skills. You are well on your way to being a communication expert! The next chapter will take rapport-building to another level as I talk about personality preferences and how changing yours to match those of others can make or break your ability to get to the truth.

7

Personality Preferences:
How to Change Yours to Meet Theirs

By now you know that people like other people who are similar to them. You have learned that you can look, sound, and act like others using the mirroring/matching rapport technique. Now let's see if you can take it a step further and adapt your personality preferences to match those of others, to deepen your personal connections.

Before you can assess the preferences of others, you first have to know your own preference style. A great way to do this is to go on-line and take a personality assessment test. I took the Myers-Briggs test initially and have based my research on Jungian type personality traits, which this chapter will focus on, but any legitimate test can be of value. Here are a few others I recommend: the DiSK Personality Assessment Tool, the Work Personality Index, the Kiersey Color Test (It Works Global uses this test), and the Birkman Color Test, just to name a few. Whichever one you choose will aid you in assessing your personality preferences and, hence, those of others. You can even study face reading, or *physiognomy*, an ancient art known around the world that I hadn't heard of until a student told me about someone named Mac Fulfer. Mac was an attorney who initially became inter-ested in face reading for the purpose of jury selection. After years of study and practice, he wrote *Amazing Face Reading*, his guide to reading faces. I had the enjoyment of speaking to Mac on the phone and through e-mails after he read my face from a photo I sent him.

He was amazing and spot on! He knew nothing yet everything about me, just from looking at my face. I was so impressed I bought his training materials. One day I hope to attend his training in person.

Knowing your personality preferences and the preferences of others will help you in several important ways. It will help prepare you to interact with people, do business, close a deal, schedule and run meetings, negotiate, deliver information, assign a task, select the right candidate for a job, mentor and coach, and so much more! It has helped me in one particular invaluable way that I will share with you in later in this chapter.

Have you ever heard of the acronym MBTI? It stands for Myers-Briggs Type Indicator. Katharine Cook-Briggs and her daughter, Isabel Briggs-Myers, studied the works and writings of Carl Gustav Jung, a Swiss psychiatrist and psychotherapist. In Jung's book *Psychological Types*, he theorized that there are four principal psychological functions by which we experience the world: sensation, intuition, feeling, and thinking, with one of these four functions prevailing most of the time. Myers and Briggs extrapolated on Jung's theory and developed their own grouping of psychological differences into four opposite pairs, or *dichotomies*, resulting in 16 possible combinations of psychological preferences. They developed a questionnaire designed to measure psychological preferences in how people get their energy (Extraversion or Introversion), how they take in information (INtuition or Sensing), how they make decisions (Thinking or Feeling), and how they organize the world around them (Judger or Perceiver). They developed this questionnaire in 1942 and called it the Briggs-Myers Type Indicator but it eventually changed names in 1956 to the Myers-Briggs Type Indicator.

The test is not meant to identify personality traits, nor does it measure or determine a person's character, morals, or values. It is meant to measure personality preferences, not aptitude. The key thing to know is that a person's personality preferences can and will change, so the MBTI measures your preferences *at the time you take the test*. Outside influences such as what kind of mood you wake up in that morning, whether or not you just experienced something traumatic, if you feel ashamed or guilty of something, or if you are ill—all will change the way you answer the questions and thus change the outcome of your score, although they won't be drastic changes. For instance, most days I am a ENTJ, meaning I prefer to get my energy from people around me (Extraversion); I like to learn information by conceptualizing and looking at the big picture before getting into details (INtuition); I make decisions based on analyzing and weighing the pros and cons, not by how it will affect other people (Thinking); and I like to order the world around me so that I complete tasks on a deadline and gain closure (Judging). However, some days, especially when I am upset, I want nothing to do with people and I just want to be alone to recharge my batteries (Introversion). Other days I get so sick and tired of rules, deadlines, and watching the clock that I just want to be spontaneous and live life with no agenda (Perception). But these days are not how I normally prefer to feel or act. If I were to take the MBTI test on a day when I didn't feel I made the best decisions or performed up to my standards, my results would differ than if I had just gotten off the stage at one of my keynote speaking events. Keep that in mind when you take the test. I will not go into an in-depth analysis of the four MBTI dichotomies, but I will give you an overview so you have an understanding of them and can identify personality preferences in yourself and others. This will help you relate to other people, communicate well with them, and, ultimately, build common ground and rapport. Following is a personal experience that will explain how all of this is possible.

In 2007, I was the project manager for a 10-week interrogation course. It was a very intensive course, and the company I worked for at the time decided to hold two of these courses almost simultaneously, with minimal staff. We were all worked to exhaustion. Because my preference is ENTJ (Extraversion, Intuition, Thinking, Judging) I was trying to organize the stressful world around me, which resulted in that Judging preference kicking into overdrive. I was creating and enforcing rules, time lines, and deadlines for both the students and staff. While I was doing this, unfortunately, I was so focused on getting the job done and providing the best training for the students that I didn't realize I was coming across as aggressive, authoritative, demanding, and even insincere to the students. The staff already knew me and probably just ignored my actions. Even though I cared about the quality of the training they were receiving, they perceived me as uncaring. My intentions never changed; I put 110-percent effort into teaching and mentoring them because I cared deeply for one goal: to prepare those students to interrogate terrorists and extract intelligence information to save lives. I didn't teach to make friends. I thought the students would feel rewarded by my determination and hard work. Unfortunately, I was wrong, and it took some ego swallowing to accept that.

One of my students, Lisa, offered me advice privately one day at the end of the course—advice that was hard to hear then, but that I am so grateful for now. She told me that she "got" me, but that I wasn't reaching all the students because I came across as overbearing and insensitive (I assumed condescending, too, but she didn't say that). And here I thought they appreciated my dedication and effort! What good was I as an instructor if I couldn't reach and inspire all of my students? At the end of our conversation, she thanked me for being an inspiration to her. After that, I felt I had lost my touch as a mentor, teacher, instructor, trainer—what I loved doing most. How did I go wrong? My dad is a professor and admired for his "school of hard knocks" teaching style. I had developed the same style. The style was good, but I needed to work on the delivery.

I went on teaching for years after that conversation, but in every class I taught, I kept what my student had told me in the back of my mind. It wasn't until I was working toward my senior instructor badge certification at the Joint Forces Intelligence School, that I dove deeply into the study of MBTI and personality type preferences and applied it in a more practical context, teaching. In order to earn my badge, I had to create a new tool to enhance learning. I wanted to combine my skills of reading body language and rapport-building with this new tool. Once I realized that there were differences in learning styles, I decided to look at MBTI and correlate my personality preferences to the preferred learning styles of my students, and then compare that with the preferred teaching styles of instructors. In my research I discovered why I didn't reach my students in that class years earlier with Lisa, and why people's perception of me didn't match up with how I was seeing myself. Lisa and I lost touch over the years following that course, just because life gets crazy and whisks you here and there, until we reconnected on Facebook. I never had the chance to tell her how that conversation changed my career as a mentor/instructor/trainer forever. When we finally reconnected she told me, "One of my daughters is named after you: Melena." I was honored and humbled. Here is what I learned from her that day: I needed to change my communication style, which was a direct result of my personality preferences.

Following are the four dichotomies of MBTI, and what I know about my personality preferences and how I change them to meet the preferences of others to enhance their learning and build rapport.

Extraversion/Introversion

The Extraversion/Introversion dichotomy tells us how we prefer to get energized. Extraverts are energized by being around activity and other people; Introverts are energized by being by themselves or with a few close friends in a quiet environment. Because I am an Extravert I speak loudly and quickly, and I sometimes get overexcited and finish the sentences of my students when I know (or think I know) what they are about to say. I didn't realize that this being perceived as disrespectful to my introverted students, whom I expected to keep up with my energy and communication style, but they couldn't. In fact, it exhausted and frustrated them to the point that they would shut down and tune me out. I learned that when I was working with introverted students, I had to speak more slowly, and "chunk" my information between pauses to give them time to process it and respond. I had to scale back my energy and excitement, and quiet my body gestures, voice, and overall demeanor so they could communicate more comfortably with me. In short, I had to be like them. Once I started to do incorporate these change in my behavior, my introverted students were much more comfortable and relaxed around me. They asked me for advice and guidance, and could understand the concepts I taught them more readily. The shift in behavior from my students was overwhelming, and it took little effort on my part to adapt a different personality that better suited the people with whom I was communicating.

INtuition/Sensing

The INtuition/Sensing dichotomy is how we prefer to take in information. INtuitives like to take on a task by conceptualizing and seeing the big-picture outcome first and then work down to identifying specific tasks. Sensors prefer to create and read specific tasks, rules, and processes to obtain the big-picture end result. For example, I loved writing this book, but when my editor gave me a packet as thick as an ice cream sandwich, with the font sizes I had to use and the image DPI requirements, I was not happy. Let me conceptualize and theorize; let them format it! Because I am an INtuitive processor of information, I get frustrated when information is handed to me in lists and procedures. And since my students were not all INtuitives like me, guess what happened? I was inadvertently frustrating my students when I delivered information, such as details for a homework assignment or exercise scenario, in a conceptual way. I figured that they could grasp conceptual ideas and break them down to itemized rules and processes, just as I could. I was wrong. Sensors prefer to be given rules and procedures first, and from there they conceptualize and theorize the outcome. In order to effectively communicate a homework assignment or testable exercise scenario I had to change the way I delivered information to reach both my INtuitive and Sensing students. Until I understood this, I lost a lot of students, unbeknownst to me, and left them to their own devices to figure out assignments for themselves. That wasn't fair to them. Once I understood I only had to present the information in a different way, my

Sensors understood my assignment and felt comfortable with how I presented it.

Here is an example. I would give a homework assignment at the end of a long day when students were packing up ready to leave, that consisted of writing a 500-word, handwritten, double-spaced biography on themselves written in the third person. My INtuitive students would hear "write an essay about yourself" and then start to consider what they wanted to divulge: the most exciting experiences, how they would capture the audience with a killer opening line, and so on. Then, two minutes later they would raise their hands and ask, "Ms. Sisco, how many words does it have to be again? Can I type it?" They tuned out all the details and rules of the assignment, just as I would have, but they had the concept down and probably already knew what they were going to write about. My Sensors were so busy concentrating on writing down the rules of the assignment that thinking about what they would write was the furthest thing from their minds. They could tell you exactly how the assignment was to be performed, all the guidelines, and when it was due, but they had no idea what they were going to write about. They would figure that out later, according to the rules and process, of course. To prevent my Sensing students from getting distracted by my INtuitive students (who kept raising their hands asking me to repeat the details and keeping everyone later in the classroom), I decided the best way for all my students to be able to process the information, using their own preferred style, was to hand out the homework assignment typed on a sheet of paper. This way, my INtuitives could read and re-read the rules while they conceptualized, and my Sensors could digest the rules fully in order to theorize on what they would write.

In order to reach all of your students, you have to vary your methods of delivering information: verbal, written, video, lecture, and so on. Try this exercise with your friends or family members, or your students, if you are a teacher. Have them write down a list of words that come to mind when you say the word "tree." INtuitive processors will write down a bunch of words similar to this: fall, Halloween, broom, kitchen, turkey, football. Where's the connection between tree and football? I see it, of course, as those are the words I picked. Sensing processors will write down words similar to this: branch, leaves, trunk, roots, moss, earth. Do you see the difference? The Sensors are still connecting to the original tree with their words; the INtuitives are writing words that seem completely unrelated. Now choose a known INtuitive and a known Sensor and have both do the assignment to demonstrate the differences between how their minds work and process information. You'll be amazed and entertained.

Thinking/Feeling

The Thinking/Feeling dichotomy tells us how we prefer to make decisions. I mentioned earlier that my former student Lisa said I was being perceived as insensitive and uncaring, because I prefer to make decisions based on facts and analysis to reach the best outcome, rather than how they make people feel. Because of this, I sometimes inadvertently hurt people's feelings. For example, when I was the project manager for the interrogation course, I had to make a decision to drop students based on the company's set performance criteria. One particular student gave it her all, and because she was smart and had a great memory, she was able to pass the written exams we administered, but she couldn't meet the expected performance criteria when it came to applying what she learned (interrogation techniques). As a result, I dropped her from the course. Her command became upset and told me that she wouldn't be able to stay in the department because I dropped her; they would have to move her elsewhere, because this training was required. They asked me to reconsider since she did well on the written exams. My response was that I couldn't graduate her and give her the credential of being a DoD certified interrogator because she couldn't do the job in a training environment, let alone down range (in an operational environment, where things get real). She would put herself and others in danger. I was not going to back down even though I liked her and wanted her to succeed. In the end I stood by my decision, along with the other instructors' recommendations. Some people thought I was being too harsh, but I would make the same decision today.

If you know you are making a decision as a Thinker and the outcome may upset others, make sure you use a few rapport techniques when informing those affected by your decision so that you are not perceived as indifferent, insensitive, or unfeeling.

Judging/Perceiving

Lastly, the Judging/Perceiving dichotomy is how we prefer to organize the world around us. I am a Judger; I like to get things done on schedule, and I like closure. I dislike leaving things unfinished, whether it is a project or a conversation. Even in this age of technology, with smartphones and iPads (I own both), I still use sticky notes to make lists for the bills I have to pay, things I have to do, and groceries I have to buy. I tried really hard to use my iPad as my organizer, but it didn't work, I went right back to my thick, heavy, leather-bound organizer and my sticky notes. (I guess that's why I prefer to read books printed on paper rather than downloaded to a tablet.) Because of my intense focus on getting the job done, I am sometimes blind to the fact it could be done a better way. I've already decided how the job will be done in my head, so when other people have ideas about changes, I am sometimes stubbornly resistant to their ideas because I don't want to change what I have already committed to doing. This trait is not conducive to a team work environment, so it is something I consciously work against every day. This is what led to my failing my students as a mentor and teacher years ago. Fortunately I now know that I can adapt and change my Judging preference to be more of a Perceiver, to enhance my interpersonal communication skills.

Unlike Judgers, Perceivers will wait until the last minute to make a decision; they like to keep their options open. They are open to ideas and change, and therefore are more flexible than rigid Judgers. Rules, time lines, and deadlines frustrate Perceivers because they don't like to feel confined or restricted. The problem Perceivers often run into is that they take too long to make a decision or heed a call to action and thus miss deadlines.

Hopefully you now have a basic understanding of the four Jungian-based preference dichotomies and how you can apply them in your life when it comes to communicating with those around you, whether in a personal or a professional setting. There are a lot of naysayers when it comes to using personality assessment tools, but I wanted to share with you how I used one and how it helped me enhance my communication skill, and it worked. After I earned my senior instructor certification, I had the chance to use the personality assessment as an enhanced communication tool at military training facilities, which made me a better instructor and mentor. Once I become knowledgeable about other tools, I'll use them, too.

You now have 10 rapport-building techniques, my five communication tips, and an understanding of how to use personality preference types to enhance your interpersonal communication skills and form strong, mutually respectful relationships. Now let's tackle the next objective: accurately reading body language and detecting deception.

·8

B Is for Baseline:
Using All Your Senses

When I joined the U.S. Navy Reserves in 1997 as a Seaman/E3, I had no idea how that decision would affect my life. It led me on an amazing journey and it's how I got to where I am today, and in part how I came to write this book. During the years I spent as an intelligence analyst and then as an intelligence officer, working for and with different agencies, my family and friends back home in Rhode Island really didn't know exactly what I was doing. They knew I was a Navy Reservist and they knew I worked in Intelligence, but outside of that they had no clue what I was being trained to do, and they never asked. I have a big family and was fortunate to grow up with most of my cousins. We were the best of friends. We hung out together and went out together—we even went on cruises together! We were as thick as thieves. So when it came time to fly the coop, I truly hated leaving my family behind, but I needed to go and experience the world, and explore California and all its diversions. But soon the military had different plans for me. I headed back East to Alexandria, Virginia, in the summer of 2001 to work at the Office of Naval Intelligence and prepare for mobilization. Being a little closer to home made trips to Rhode Island easier, both logistically and financially.

On one particular visit home for a Christmas holiday, one of my cousins, Darren, was hosting a big-time poker game. He had a legit gambling room in his basement, equipped with a gorgeous poker table and full bar; yes, he was that serious about the game. Anyway, my brothers invited me to go over and play poker with my cousins, and wanted me to use my "mind reading skills" (which you and I both know I don't have) on Darren to beat him, because no one else could and they were all tired of losing to him. I laughed at their ignorance about my skills but went along with the plan. When I arrived, Darren warned me, "Lena, we play for money, and I am unbeatable." I smiled and asked for a cheat sheet card because I often got confused at what the hands were and which ones beat each other. "Are you serious?" he asked, laughing. Then this huge grin came over his face as he realized I was an easy target; he was going to take my money and bounce me out of the game—or so he thought!

I bought in and kept my cheat sheet close by as we started to play (because I seriously didn't know how to play poker). Darren was good. He was winning almost every hand. Meanwhile I watched him closely. I studied his eyes, facial expressions, and gestures when he first looked at his cards, when he won on a good hand, and when he won on a bluff. Eight of us started out playing that night. After a couple hours it came down to Darren and me. Everyone was shocked I was still in the game, especially since I still was using my cheat sheet. I must admit, though, that I purposefully played up my naiveté to make everyone think I was just a dumb girl trying to play poker— certainly no threat. I kept their focus off me, so they never studied my reactions. I knew when Darren had a good hand because he would frown slightly and his body gestures quieted down; he would concentrate. I think he was concentrating on trying to not show his tells! When he didn't have a good hand he would smile nervously, become fidgety with his cards, reposition himself in his chair, and became more talkative; he would even taunt me, almost as though he were trying too hard to appear confident: overcompensating.

So there we were, both of us holding our cards, getting ready to show our hands. With contempt written all over his face, Darren said, "Lena, you played a good game, but unfortunately, you won't be taking home that pot of money tonight." (I will talk more about contempt in the next chapter.) What I noticed was that he couldn't look at me when he said this; his eyes darted around the room and he started shuffling his cards. I knew he was bluffing. "Read 'em and weep!" he said, as he threw down his cards. There on the table were two kings and one queen. I looked at him, sighed, and placed my cards down very slowly, one by one, "Well, shoot, those are good cards, Darren—but mine are better." There on the table were two kings and an ace. Everyone cheered and laughed in amazement. Darren was so shocked he was speechless. "I guess that $220 is mine, right?" I gave half to my youngest brother because I felt badly he had lost.

They still call me a mind reader, but you know I'm not, and neither will you be. You will not always be 100-percent accurate, and you will not always win every game of poker. There is a margin of error when detecting deception, but this margin is slender when it comes to people who have had years of experience reading body language, interpreting behavioral congruency, and listening for verbal deceptive tells. To really bring that margin of error down, you need to use all you sense, especially your eyes and ears, when people talk. We listen to the words they say and match them to how they are said (voice pitch, tone, word usage), and whether the body is in agreement or not. I started off this book by telling you detecting deception was hard, and it is. You have to really focus and pay attention to pick up on the subtle clues and tells people will leak, and then compare what is being said verbally to what the body is saying nonverbally, and all with precise timing!

Follow the Rule of Three (or, Don't Read Me)

The key to being a good lie detector is baselining people's body language before you can say they are leaking deceptive tells. Here is my rule of three when it comes to detecting deception: 1) baseline a person's normal behavior (how they normally act, carry themselves, move, gesture, talk, sound, and speak); 2) identify clusters of deceptive tells (verbal or nonverbal), because only one deceptive tell is not enough to determine whether someone is lying; and 3) know the context in which the information is being delivered (meaning, is the person stressed, under duress, hurt, not feeling well, on medications, and so on, because all of these factors can affect their body language).

1. Baseline

So, how do you baseline people? First, hold a 15-minute conversation with them when they are relaxed, calm, and comfortable with you and their surroundings. Talk about casual, non-pertinent topics; don't bombard them with questions, and don't allow them to control the conversation. Make them feel relaxed and at ease so you can see how they normally act. Then, study them closely and observe the following:

- **Stance and posture:** Do they slouch or stand up straight? Are the shoulders rolled back or rolled forward? Do they shift weight frequently or stand still? Do they use power poses? (Review Chapter 5 if you need a refresher on these.)

- **Feet:** Do they point them toward you or away from you when they are talking? Do they tap their feet or keep them still? Do they cross their ankles while they sit or stand? Do they rise up on their toes or remain flat-footed when they speak?

- **Hands:** Do they talk with their hands? Do they wring them, hide them in their pockets, touch their face with them or touch you, relax them in their laps, show you their palms or keep them hidden? Do they pick at their cuticles?

- **Eyes:** Do they make good eye contact or do their eyes dart around? Do they blink frequently, stare, roll their eyes, or raise their eyebrows? Where do their eyes go when they are trying to recall information? (I'll talk more about neurolinguistic programming (NLP) later in Chapter 9.)

- **Mouth:** Do they smile a lot or frown? Do they bite, purse, or lick their lips?

- **Voice:** Is their voice high- or low-pitched? Loud or soft and deep?

- **Speech:** What kinds of words do they use? Softening (more on this in Chapter 10), visual, kinesthetic, descriptive, negative, or positive? What is their normal rate of speech?

Once you have a good idea of how they move their body and how they speak, start to ask pertinent questions to see if you notice any shifts in their normal behavior. (I will teach you good questioning techniques in Chapter 10.) To give you an idea of how this works, I will share my baseline with you—just don't use it against me! I am half Italian, I am from Rhode Island, and I am an Extravert. I speak loudly and quickly, and I am very animated; I talk with my hands. In fact, I have to have something moving at all times, whether I'm tapping my feet, gesturing with my hands, or twirling my hair. I have very expressive eyes and eyebrows. Also, I am very personable so I may touch your upper arm frequently when we talk (if I like you). If I suddenly become quiet, stop moving, self-preen, or avert eye contact, you'll know something is wrong, because my normal behavior has just changed. Now you have to figure out why. Is it because I am stressed about the topic you brought up? Or did I just lie to you as I answered your question?

Exercise: Baseline Yourself

Stand in front of a mirror and say something that is truthful. Then tell a lie. Talk about something that makes you sad and then something that makes you happy. While you do this, observe your face. Do you see emotions leaking out? What is your mouth doing? What do your eyes and eyebrows show? If you feel funny and can't do this exercise without laughing, ask a friend to observe you, but tell her what to look for. Think about how you act when you comfortable and when you are stressed.

---

2. Clusters

As I mentioned, the presence of just one tell can't determine deception. You need to see more evidence, at least three or four tells, to help you decide whether or not a person is lying to you. And then you have to confirm the lie by getting the truth. I will teach you numerous nonverbal deceptive tells in Chapter 9, and verbal deceptive tells in Chapter 10. Once you have your collection of tells you'll be able to look for clusters of them.

I still train DoD personnel in elicitation and elicitation countermeasures, and I am used as a role player for elicitation training exercises. During one training event, I was sent to approach a student to elicit information from him; my goal was to collect basic biographical information such as his name, address, employment, occupation, and so on. I approached my target and started an unassuming, friendly conversation. I extended my hand and said, "By the way, my name is Lena." Predictably, he shook my hand and said, "My name is [and here he paused] John," as he broke eye contact and looked down. At one point in our conversation I said to him, "I can tell you're not from here." (I didn't want to ask him point blank where he was from, because it could have raised some concern as to why I wanted to know, so I used an elicitation technique instead.) He broke eye contact again, looked at his drink, took a hard swallow, took a sip of the drink, sighed, looked back at me and said, "I'm from Arizona?"

"Really?" I responded doubtfully.

He looked surprised and became defensive. "Yeah, why?"

I replied, "Oh, it sounded like you were unsure."

"No, I'm from Arizona."

Well, he wasn't, and as a trained body-language expert I knew he wasn't. The reason I knew this was because he displayed a cluster of tells: (1) he broke eye contact, (2) he swallowed hard (which could indicate that his mouth was drying out from stress), (3) he sighed (a calming response), and (4) he made a statement using an inflection. These four tells pretty much told me that he was lying. I later found out he was from Pennsylvania, and of course his name wasn't John. I knew that, too, because who pauses to think when asked their name?

3. Context

The third rule states that you have to consider the context in which you are receiving information from someone in order to accurately assess deception. For example, trauma, shock, sickness, stress, distress, and intoxication are factors that can greatly influence how a person communicates, both verbally and nonverbally. You may perceive certain nonverbal "tells" to be deceptive when they are actually just a result of fear. Context affects verbal tells, as well. If someone just had dental work, suffers from severe TMJ (as I do), has a sore throat, is hoarse from yelling at a concert the night before, is a heavy smoker, or is on an antidepressant or muscle relaxer, all of these factors can change patterns and rate of speech, as well as volume, tone, and pitch of voice.

When detainees would arrive from Bagram, Afghanistan, to Guantanamo Bay, Cuba, they did so by plane. Most Afghans and the foreign fighters fighting in Afghanistan for al Qaeda and the Taliban had never been on a plane before. So you can imagine that many were fearful of flying; most got motion sickness. After a long flight from Afghanistan to Cuba, they were then put on a ferry, then a bus, and then driven to the prison camp where they were screened medically, washed, issued their prison attire and accoutrements, and ushered into an interrogation booth for about 20 to 30 minutes to be questioned. I was one of those initial interrogators. We wanted to get a quick assessment of who had information of intelligence value and who was most likely to be willing to give us that information in the least amount of time. This usually meant identifying the detainees who required the least amount of effort from us regarding interrogation plans, focused questioning techniques, elicitation, and approaches. During this 30-minute interrogation it was very difficult for me to detect deception because I was seeing their stress, shock, and anxiety from the ordeal they just went through to get there. Some were throwing up in a garbage can, and others were just plain exhausted, so it made no sense to me to try and assess their truthfulness and accuracy at that point. I collected information but would have to check it for truthfulness and accuracy later, after they had settled in for a day or two and I could conduct a full interrogation.

Now you know my rule of three when it comes to detecting deception: baseline first, look for clusters of tells, and know the context in which you are observing those tells. In the next chapter I am going to talk about how to spot deviations from the baseline, and how this can help you detect deception.

9

L Is for Look for Deviations: Behavioral Incongruence

In this chapter I will provide you with a framework for observing body language—postures, gestures, and facial expressions—the meanings they often carry, and how they can indicate deception. When reading body language, you need to look at the entire body, from the feet to the forehead, so make sure you can see the entire body when you're observing someone.

When I was training Department of Defense personnel, I would sometimes sit in the back of the room and observe the students (who had no idea yet who I was) during an exercise we created for them called "Impromptus." Each student would be required to stand in front of the class and defend a random, controversial, and even embarrassing opinion that he or she did not actually hold for two minutes, trying to convince the class on his or her stance. For instance, one student might have to defend why women should not be allowed in the military; another might defend why cheating on your spouse is okay. Putting the students in front of the classroom made them nervous enough, but forcing them to defend a topic they were not only uncomfortable with, but completely disagreed with, added even more pressure and stress. I would observe the intense stress in their body language, making sure I could see everything from their feet to their foreheads, and document all the tells I saw in each. Once the exercises concluded, the instructor would say, "While you were doing this, a body language expert was sitting in the back of the class observing your tells. Let me introduce your next instructor, who will be teaching you behavioral congruency." At that I would see a whole slew of tells, including rapid eye blinking, hard swallowing, pacing, self-preening, expressive eye movements, thumbs of power, feet facing toward the door with torso facing the class, hiding hands, and micro-expressions leaking from the face. These tells were coming from nerves, anxiety, and—yes—deception. The purpose of the exercise was two fold: first, I wanted to inform the students of their tells because of what would be expected of them in their professional careers; and second, I wanted to teach them what to look for in other people, and to know that these tells could be the result of deception or anxiety or both.

The body can "leak" deception through the face (expressions), the head, the eyes, the mouth, the hands, signs of uncertainty, and the nose (what I call the Pinocchio effect). Start to look for these tells in the people you feel are being deceptive with you. But remember my golden rule of three: baseline first, look for clusters of tells, and know the context in which you are seeing these tells. I like to see at least three tells, all at once or back-to-back, before I make the determination that someone is being deceitful. One tell alone is not enough to determine deception; this is what the "mind readers" do, and why they are so often wrong.

The Face: Emotions and Facial Leakage

Human emotions are universal, meaning no matter what continent you are on, what country you are in, or what subculture you are dealing with, every human being shows emotions the same way through facial expressions. Dr. Paul Ekman, an American psychologist and human lie detector, who also served as the scientific advisor to the TV series *Lie to Me*, is considered to be the pioneer of research regarding human emotions and how they are depicted through facial expressions. His research took him to Papua New Guinea, where he proved human emotions are expressed the same universally.

Dr. Ekman wanted to prove that emotions were biologically determined and not culturally adapted. In his early research he came up with six basic emotions: happiness, sadness, surprise, anger, fear, and disgust. He later added contempt, but there are many other sub-emotions, as well: worry, guilt, shame, embarrassment, jealousy, love, relief, curiosity, and more. So why do you need to know what human emotions look like? Because when you learn to detect deception, you will need to be able to tell the difference between real and fake emotions, what true emotions people are trying to hide, and what fake emotions they are trying to portray. And, as the saying goes, you don't know what you don't know.

When someone experiences an emotion or emotions, the muscles in the face respond and depict those emotions outwardly. A true emotion will linger on the face in a corresponding facial expression that lasts for a few seconds. These expressions are called *macro-expressions*; they indicate truthfulness and sincerity. When people are supressing true emotions, either deliberately or unconsciously, they will still leak out in the form of *micro-expressions*, a term coined by Dr. Ekman. Micro-expressions flash across the face for a fraction of second and are very hard to detect. You will never see them if you aren't paying attention, which is why it is critical to be on high alert when you are trying to detect deception. There are a lot of "moving parts" to the art and science of detecting deception. It is both an art and science because the finesse and expertise required to notice clusters of tells and decipher what they mean is an art form, while deciphering the biological and physiological responses that occur when people lie is a kind of science. Observing facial micro-expressions is a good tool for detecting deception, but remember: One expression by itself if not enough. You need more.

Following are the physical attributes of the seven basic emotions I listed previously, with corresponding photos. Learn what they look like (or what they should look like) so you can spot them on the faces of others. Once you learn how these emotions show up physically in the face, you'll start to pick up on them more easily. Study people's faces; practice makes perfect.

1. **Anger.** Here you can see the eyebrows are furrowed, brought down and together; the eyes are fixed steadily, almost glaring; and the lips are tightly pursed.

2. **Fear.** When people are afraid, they will raise their eyebrows and sometimes pinch them together. Their eyes widen, but the lower eyelids will tense up and seem to move upward. Their lips will separate and draw back as the jaw tightens. People may show fear in a micro-expression when you have discovered their lie.

3. **Disgust.** When people feel dislike or disgust, they will wrinkle their nose as if they just smelled a skunk. The eyebrows will furrow together, so you will see wrinkling in the forehead, and the corners of the mouth will turn down. So ladies, if you ask your husband, boyfriend, or significant other whether he likes your new asymmetrical haircut, and he looks at you, scrunches his nose, and says, "Yeah, it's cute," he's probably just being kind.

4. **Surprise.** Surprise looks a lot like fear, but if you look closely you will see there are major differences. When people are surprised they will raise their eyebrows, but they won't pinch them together. The eyes open up wide, just as they do in fear, but in this case they are more rounded because the lower eyelid stays separate. Sometimes you can even see the whites of the eyes surrounding the entire pupil. The mouth will open and lower jaw will drop open. Everyone in the world shows surprise in this was. Let's say you are pretty sure your wife is having an affair, and you are pretty sure you know whom with, so when you ask her, "Sandra, have you seen Tom lately?" and she shows surprise, you'd better sit her down for a heart-to-heart conversation. She may be showing surprise because you think she's having an affair, or she may be showing surprise because you found out she's actually having one!

Anger.

Fear.

Disgust.

Surprise.

Happiness.

Sadness.

Contempt.

5. **Happiness.** True happiness is expressed in a genuine smile that reaches the eyes. So you should see lines and wrinkles (crow's feet) around the eyes when someone genuinely smiles. You can often see models and movie stars flashing their pearly whites in a fake smile to avoid causing crow's feet. I admit I do the same thing. People will smile when they are happy, when they are embarrassed, and when they feel like they are getting away with a lie. Some people smile uncontrollably, in a micro-expression, when they lie. My detainees used to try to literally wipe the smiles off their faces when they lied to me. Jodi Arias and Neil Entwistle, both convicted murderers, have been seen on TV in court "crying." But strangely there are no tears—no true sadness. If you look closely, what you can see behind the facial blocking, as they cover their faces with their hands as they pretend to cry, is the corners of the mouths turning up in a tiny smile. This may seem an obvious statement, but if they were truly that sad, the corners of their mouths would turn down, not up; they simply weren't able to control their true emotion leaking out—their happiness. This is called *duping delight*, another Paul Ekman term. It refers to a smile that flashes across the face when someone is hiding something or getting away with something (or so they think).

6. **Sadness.** True sadness is seen in the mouth, the eyes, the eyebrows, and even the chin! When someone is sad, the corners of their mouths will turn down, *always*. The inner eyebrows will often pinch upward and together, as well. Sometimes the chin will dimple, especially when tears are imminent. For those of you who have children, look at them the next time they are about to cry and notice what you see; then notice what you don't see when they are shedding crocodile tears.

7. **Contempt.** When I ask people to define contempt, most can't. Contempt is the feeling of superiority, moral or otherwise—the "I'm better than you" feeling. When someone leaks contempt, it means he feels superior in some way. It is usually seen in a simple half-smile; one side of the mouth turns up, while the other doesn't. The question we have to ask ourselves when we see contempt is: *Why* does this person feel so superior?

Most people have no idea that they leak emotions. When I spot micro-expressions, or what I call facial leakage, I will tell the other person, but often they won't believe me. One occurrence of facial leakage that I'll always remember occurred when I was observing the Impromptus exercise I mentioned earlier. One woman got up in front of the room to talk about how much she hated her mother and how awful of a person she was. As she paced back and forth, talking to the floor and hardly making eye contact with any of us, I was studying her body language closely. At one point, I saw the corners of her mouth turn down for a split second before she glanced up and continued to try to convince the class that her mother was a negative influence in her life. After she was done, I said to her, "You love your mother!" (Remember that I didn't know if she had grown up with a mother or even a mother figure; I knew nothing about her or her family.) She looked at me and almost teared up: "Yes! I hated saying those horrible things!" I told her she leaked true sadness for a split second and I saw it. She had no idea. Sometimes our emotions are so strong they come out no matter how hard we try to hide them.

Here are four short case studies on identifying facial micro-expressions. In one, it helped identify and ultimately address a problem a Marine had; in another, it helped a weapons trainer win a contract with food; in the third, it helped an interrogator obtain a confession from a terrorist; and in the last one, it proved that we all leak them. Note that all names and identifying details (including titles and jobs) have been changed to protect privacy.

Case study # 1: Micro-expressions and the CI guy

A major (Maj) in the United States Marine Corp (USMC) who was the executive officer of a particular unit in a USMC organization invited a young sergeant (Sgt) into his office to ask him about how he liked working for this particular unit. The major had a concern that the sergeant was unhappy. Here is the dialogue that ensued:

Maj: "How do you like working here?"

Sgt: "I love it, sir." [*This was followed by more enthusiastic assent.*]

Maj: "Sergeant, do you know my background?"

Sgt: "Yes, sir. You are a CI guy." [*CI stands for counter intelligence.*]

Maj: "Correct. That means I am trained to read people. When I just asked you that question, a split second before you answered, you leaked the facial expression of disgust."

[*The sergeant sat there quietly staring at the major.*]

Maj: "So, I am going to ask you that question again: How do you like working here?"

Sgt: [*A pause, then a sigh*] "I hate it, sir."

Case study # 2: Micro-expressions and hunger pains

Nic, a partner and lead weapons and tactics instructor for Weaponcraft, LLC, and a former Marine student of mine, found me on Facebook and contacted me recently to thank me for my class on body language he attended years ago. He wanted to share a success story with me to tell me how my training helped him win a big contract for his company. Here is his story:

> During a recent business meeting I found myself teamed against a potentially powerful new client with a seriously short attention span. As I went through my normal rapport- building song and dance, I could see I was getting nowhere. I'm talking crickets, like, I've seen a more lively group at the DMV.

While I worked through my presentation I realized that I was losing my client completely and knew I only had a short time to build some rapport before this whole meeting was going to be a wash. I started looking him over for a clue as to what was wrong and how I could fix it. Was I boring? Did he not like my PowerPoint? Maybe I've got bad breath? Once I cognitively started looking, it became all too obvious.

My client, who initially was sitting across from me, had rotated his chair and pointed his entire body toward the nearest exit, aside from his craned neck. His head was shaking side-to-side signifying "no" even though he was vocalizing "yes." Then his hands started dancing across the desk, and his fingers were performing a tandem ice-skating routine— that is, until he found his pen. His fixation [on] that pen could be related to the first time man discovered fire—not looking good for me landing this client. Luckily I was running late to my meeting that day, and because of that, I didn't have time to fully clean up from my lunch. As I was pondering, trying to build rapport with this guy so he didn't walk out, I picked up my half-eaten sandwich and went to throw it in the trash. With that, all my questions were answered.

When the client saw my food and [the fact] that I was about to throw it in the trash, his eyes widened like dinner plates. My client wasn't bored, [and] he didn't think I was a bad choice to lead his project; he was hungry. I quickly asked if he would like to finish the conversation over a cup of coffee at the restaurant across the street; he barely had his response out before he had grabbed his coat and headed for the door. Within five minutes of my client getting some food, the deal was done, and he was a completely and much more pleasant person. There is no doubt in my mind if I hadn't been able to pick up his subtle clues, I would have never spoken to him again once he left that room.

Case study # 3: Micro-expressions and a terrorist's confession

It was around 1100 hours on a warm September day in 2002 in Cuba. I had just walked into my air-conditioned interrogation booth with my Pashtu linguist assigned to me for that day. As we waited for our Afghani detainee to be escorted to the booth, the sweat started to freeze on my body. He arrived in chains and the standard-issue orange detainee jumpsuit. He had a pleasant demeanor and engaged in conversation with us willingly. As the interrogation progressed, I began to notice that every time I said "al Qaeda," he would cover his mouth to hide a smile. There was confirmed intelligence that he was a member, so I was just trying to get confirmation from him. After his numerous attempts to hide his smile (duping delight), I finally leaned in and asked, "Do you know that every time I say al Qaeda, you laugh?" He started smiling, and, again, the hand went to his mouth. "No, no," he said. I told him, "Sometimes when people lie, they smile and laugh because they are either embarrassed, thinking they will get caught, or they are happy, thinking they are getting away with it. Which one are you?" He finally admitted to being a member, but insisted he had done nothing wrong.

Case study # 4: micro-expressions and a concerned detainee

In GTMO I experienced my very first panic attack. It happened during an interrogation—a boring one, actually. As I listened to a detainee, my heart suddenly decided to flip out. It started beating super-fast and hard, so fast that I couldn't catch my breath. Even thought I was trying to act as though everything was okay, I must have had a look of surprise on my face, because my detainee said something, and my interpreter leaned over and said, "He wants to know if you are all right." My heart went back to beating normally and I replied, "I hope so! My heart started beating really fast." He replied, "I hope you are okay." I was amazed that he had seen the emotion on my face, not to mention that he had any concern for me.

Now you can see how being able to read facial expressions—and better yet, being able to identify them in a split second to uncover someone's true emotions—can change the outcome of a difficult situation.

The Head

One of the easiest ways to see behavioral congruence or incongruence is to look at what the head does, especially when someone is saying yes or no. Typically, if someone is being truthful, there will be congruence between what she is saying and what her body is telling you. However, if she is saying yes, but shakes her their head side-to-side to indicate no, listen to what her head is saying, not her lips. You need to figure out why there is such incongruence here. Lance Armstrong provided a perfect example of behavioral incongruence when he was interviewed under oath about his use of performance-enhancing drugs by SCA Promotions attorney Jeffrey Tillotson. This was in 2005, before he finally admitted he had been doping for years to win the Tour de France. At one point Tillotson asked Lance, "Do you deny...the statements Miss Andrews attributed to you in the Indiana University hospital?" (Betsy Andrews was a nurse who worked at the hospital; in her deposition she stated that Lance made statements while he was in the hospital about taking performance-enhancing drugs.) In response, Lance shook his head no (he moved his head side-to-side) as he said, "One hundred percent, absolutely." His words and his body language didn't match up; there was serious incongruence. Lance exhibited another verbal deceptive tell: He didn't answer yes or no to a yes-or-no question; instead he answered "Absolutely." "Absolutely" is not a substitute for yes or no! (I'll talk more about deceptive substitutions in answers to yes-or-no questions in Chapter 10.) Lance also said "100-percent." Why did he feel the need to add that qualifier? He didn't use it when he answered the other questions. Liars tend to use this phraseology to convince us of their lies. Again, one tell alone didn't prove he was lying, but he gave us three of them—a very good indication that he was being deceptive. (And, of course, the truth all came out later anyway.) I'll discuss verbal deceptive tells in greater depth in Chapter 10.

Lying Eyes

The eye is the window of the soul, the mouth the door.
The intellect, the will, are seen in the eye; the emotions,
sensibilities, and affections, in the mouth. The animals
look for man's intentions right into his eyes. Even a rat,
when you hunt him and bring him to bay, looks you in
the eye.

—Hiram Powers

Eye contact

The eyes can show emotions, intentions, thoughts, and feelings. I am a huge animal lover; I have (too) many of my own; my friends and family think I'm crazy. For three years I was a volunteer zookeeper aid at a local AZA zoo, and I currently volunteer at another AZA institution, taking care of program animals and handling large birds of prey. I have worked with tigers, binturong, tapir, bears, primates, kangaroos, birds of prey, otters, prairie dogs, red river hogs, antelope, various hoof stock, owls, kestrels, and rabbits. I have learned that eye contact with animals plays just as an important role as it does with humans. For example, you should never look a tiger directly in the eyes, because the tiger will take it as a sign of aggression and think you are trying to provoke a fight. You definitely want to avoid that, and I'm speaking from experience. I'll never forget the first day I met two new young Siberian tigers. It was early in the morning and they were still in their inside enclosure, waiting to be let outside so they could frolic in the pond and play with their favorite beach balls. I walked into the enclosure along with the keeper who worked with them. They were familiar with her but not with me. She knelt down on the ground, so I knelt beside her. As I did I caught the eye of one of the boy tigers, and he locked on to me. I just couldn't tear my eyes away, probably because I knew what was about to happen and didn't want to miss it. He lowered his head, opened his mouth, and began to pace back and forth. Then he jumped up on the cage door, which was only about three feet away from me. Talk about scary! I was a new potential threat in his domain. After a few weeks had passed, they had seen me a few more times since the incident. It was Saturday mid-morning and we had just let them out to their outside enclosure. After we cleaned the inside enclosure I went to check on them outside through a hidden metal door that the public can't see. They both saw me at the door and came running up. I thought, *Oh crap. I pissed them off again!* But what happened next really shocked me. They pranced around the door, playing with each other like two big domestic cats, and then started rubbing their faces on the gate, just as my cat Titus does at home to mark his territory (usually that's me and the furniture). I knelt down again, but this time instead of charging me, they were chuffing (a sound of pleasure and greeting). So I started chuffing back at them. It was incredibly cool, but I never doubted for a second that those big kitties could toss me around like a cat toy if they had the chance.

Hiram Powers said animals look for our intentions in our eyes. If you look a strange dog in the eye, it will look back to see whether you are scared or aggressive. It may attack either way: If you are vulnerable, it won't be intimidated by you; but if you seem aggressive, it will want to defend itself. If you're unsure of the animal, it's better to look at its nose or ears. Currently, I have been experimenting with the blink rates of the screech owls I work with. I have found that they will mimic my blink rate and even the length of the blink, fast or slow, long or short. It's amazing! I do this as a de-stressing technique before I handle them. It works, but I don't know why yet. That's my next research project!

In the United States we are taught that it's respectful to make good eye contact. But staring weightily or glaring at someone is just rude and awkward. Good eye contact involves looking in the eyes, around the face, and breaking contact every so often. Do what feels comfortable and normal for you.

There are a lot of misconceptions regarding the eyes and lying. You will typically hear that breaking eye contact means that someone is lying. I actually find that to be true in most people, but not all. Some liars will give you a hard stare. They do this because they are aware of the fact that liars are thought to have shifty eyes, and so they purposely strive not to break eye contact and end up staring. Both staring and shiftiness can be indicators of deception, particularly when they represent a departure from someone's baseline behavior, so remember to baseline a person's eye movements before you start to make any judgment calls.

Eye movement is a normal activity when we are talking. Staring people down is considered rude and even hostile, even in the United States. In other cultures, however, it is rude to make any direct eye contact. I found this out when I was in Korea. So make sure you know the cultural norms of your surroundings. As a former archaeologist I had this base knowledge prior to my life as an interrogator, so I had an advantage of knowing about cultural norms and sensitivities. The important thing is to do what feel natural to you while still respecting the feelings and expectations of those around you.

Rapid eye blinking

People who get nervous and anxious when they lie will experience the physiological responses I talked about in Chapter 5. One of those responses is that the eyes start to dry out. A result of this is the tell of rapid eye blinking, which occurs in an effort to lubricate the eyes. Bill Clinton blinked rapidly throughout his grand jury testimony, when he lied about his intimate relationship with Monica Lewinsky. Was he nervous? Most likely. Was he lying? Yes, he was. Did the rapid eye blinking indicate nervousness or deception? In his case, I would say both. He was nervous from lying under oath. His testimony was littered with clusters of deceptive tells, some of which I will cover in the next chapter. I see instructors on the platform blinking like this when they are nervous. Unless there is something caught in your eye, like an eyelash or an out-of-place contact lens, or there is a physical aliment such as pink eye, rapid eye blinking definitely indicates anxiety and is a good indication of deception in those people who get nervous when they lie (which is most of us).

Prolonged blinking

When people blink at you slowly, it's usually a sign of an emotional response or concentration. They could be experiencing a strong emotion, which is causing them to shut their eyes. They could be putting up a mental block up against something they heard and didn't like, almost as though closing their eyes would protect them from whatever it was they found disturbing. They could be preparing to tell a lie and trying to think of what to say. Or, it could be that they just don't want to look you in the eye as they lie (because remember: The eyes are the gateway to the soul). There are too many possible meanings behind a prolonged eye blink, but stacked up against other clusters of deceptive tells, it may be an indicator of deception.

Neuro-linguistic programming (NLP)

The use of NLP as a tool for detecting deception is controversial. Scientists, psychologists, and NLP certified trainers alike all refute the idea that NLP can be used to monitor eye movements to detect deception. The NLP theory, just like the Myers-Briggs Personality Preference Dichotomies, is said to be poorly supported scientifically, and that the initial research contained factual errors and thus has been discredited by the scientific community. I believe this is because it is not taught correctly. I like using NLP to help detect deception, and I will tell you why and how. But first, I am going to give you a very brief history on NLP in layperson's terms.

Let's first dissect the term. You can see that it has three distinct components: neurology, language, and programming. Neurology has to do with how our brains function—how we think. Language is what it sounds like—how we communicate. And programming has to do with managing our thought patterns and our mental and emotional behaviors. The notion that certain eye movements are related to specific thought patterns was first suggested by American psychologist William James in his 1890 book, *Principles of Psychology*. It wasn't until the early 1970s, however, that psychologists began to link eye movements to different cognitive processes associated with the two brain hemispheres. In 1976, John Grinder and Richard Bandler further explored the relationship among neurology, language, and programming, and how this relationship could be used to achieve specific goals in life. It was Bandler and Grinder who claimed the science of NLP could treat problems such as eating and learning disorders, phobias, and unwanted habits and behaviors, just to name a few.

Grinder and Bandler also created the eye accessing cue chart. This chart links the direction of someone's gaze to how that person is thinking, or what sense that person is engaging. Grinder and Bandler say that our life experiences are catalogued in our minds and are recalled by their association with an experience or a sense: visual (sight), auditory (hearing), kinesthetic (emotional, but includes touch), olfactory (smell), and gustatory (taste). In NLP these senses are referred to as *modalities*. For example, when I smell a certain scented candle I am instantly taken back to late 1980s when my best friend, Tina, and I would spend endless carefree summer days at the beaches in Rhode Island. In this case the olfactory sense triggers the memory.

According the chart:

- If a person looks up, he is accessing the visual senses, either to recall information (up and to the left) or create/construct information (up and to the right).

- If someone looks at about ear level, he is accessing the auditory senses to recall information (to the left) or create/construct information (up and to the right).

- If a person looks down and to the left, he is accessing the kinesthetic senses; feelings both recalled and constructed. If he looks down and to the right, he is engaging in an internal dialogue, essentially talking to himself. About what? That's for you to figure out.

These are all general guidelines and not meant to be taken as absolutes. As they say, your mileage will vary.

The problem with using NLP as a deception-detecting tool is twofold. First, it's not an absolute, hard-and-fast science, as different people may respond differently, with different eye movements, based on how they are wired. For example, I don't look up and the left when accessing memories; I usually look straight in front of me, unless I am really trying to remember something like dates (which I am awful with), at which point I will usually look up and to the left. So realize that people may not be assessing or constructing the information where they are "supposed" to be, according to the chart. Second, there can be multiple eye cues in any one response. Sometimes you can observe a strong initial emotional response before the person goes to logic and reason, or vice versa. Moreover, even when people lie they tend to access some truth, and this will show up in the eye movements, as well. For example, if a teenager wanted to lie about why he came home past curfew last night and say it was because his friend's car broke down, an image of his friend's dilapidated car may really exist in his mind, so he will recall the image of the car and his eyes will go up and to the left (visual recall). Of course, he still may feel guilty and sad about lying, so his eyes may go down and to the right (kinesthetic, emotional feelings). And, if he suddenly remembers that time his parents' car broke down and his father started yelling, his eyes may go straight and to the left (auditory recall). Notice that never once during this lie did the teenager's eyes go up and to the right (visual construct), which would have been a clear sign that he was making stuff up. And finally, remember that you can't use NLP by itself to detect deception; you need to baseline and look for clusters of other deceptive tells.

There is a secret I share with my students to get a baseline in less than a minute: If you want to know where someone's eyes go to recall information, ask this question: "What is the sixth word in the Star Spangled Banner?" Nine out of 10 people go up and to the left as they respond. (The other one out of 10 will stare straight at me because they have no idea why I pulled them in front of the room for everyone to watch.) They are literally singing the song in their head and counting the words. So, if I asked someone, "How much debt do you owe?" and she looked up and to the right as she said, "About $5,000," it could mean she constructed that number (maybe because she is embarrassed about how much she really owes). I would then dig deeper into that question and exploit it further to see if she were being truthful or not. A good follow-up question is simply "Really?" a questioning technique I'll discuss further in the next chapter.

During Janine Driver's Body Language Institute's "Train the Trainer" weeklong program (10-plus-hour days), we conduct an exercise in which every student tells a truthful story to the class so we can baseline their verbal and nonverbal behavior, including eye movement. Then they tell two additional stories, one that's true and one that's made up. I caught one student's lie fairly easily because her eye movements deviated so blatantly from her baseline. I didn't use that clue alone to determine she was lying, of course; that would have been foolish. I saw other deceptive tells that I was able to group in a cluster, but the deviation in her eye movements was one of the clearest indications that she was lying. I was able to determine which story was true and which one was the whopper.

Once you get a baseline, you need to test it. Ask questions you already know the answers to. Ask questions that would make the respondent recall images, sounds, and feelings. Then ask him questions that would require him to construct an image, a sound, or a feeling. For example, for vision recall and construct, you could ask, "What does the inside of a UFO look like?" followed by "Describe your living room." For audio recall and construct, you could ask, "What sound would a pterodactyl make?" followed by "Now describe the sound of a baby crying." For kinesthetic recall and construct of feelings, you could ask, "How would you feel if X happened?" I will tell you a secret: Liars won't have feelings associated with their lie, because it never happened. They will have to make up feelings that they think they *should* have had. So if you suspect your teenager is lying about why he came home late, ask him, "How did that make you feel?" If he is lying, he will hesitate by using a filler word or some other stalling technique. Remember: If it didn't happen, he will have to imagine a feeling he thinks he should have had. This is actually one of my go-to questions when I think people are lying. And finally, if during a conversation you see someone looking down and to the left, she may be having an internal conversation or debate as to whether she ought to lie or not, weighing pros and cons. If you think this is happening, ask, "What's on your mind?" Watch her eyes and where they go. Responses to both of the questions involve recalling information, so in both cases the eyes should be going to same area. If they don't, you'll need to find out why.

The Mouth

Swallowing hard

Just like rapid eye blinking, hard swallowing is the body's response to drying out from stress. You can hear when people's mouths dry out, in the raspy voice, and you can see it in the hard swallows and the spit that dries around the mouth. Hard swallowing indicates anxiety and nerves, and, taken with other tells, it can be indicative of deception, as well.

Disappearing lips

As Janine Driver says, "When we don't like what we hear, our lips disappear." If you Google pictures of Anthony Weiner that were taken when he was lying about his sexting, you can often see a clenched jaw and tight lips. If someone insistently denies something but purses his lips as he does so, he is likely pretty unhappy about whatever it is he is being accused of. My mom has naturally thin lips, but when she's mad, she has none!

The Hands

Hiding hands

People think by putting their hands in their pockets they appear more casual and relaxed, but it is actually a message of nervousness. Anytime you hide a body part, especially the hands, you are hiding how you feel. If you hide your hands, you hide your emotions. You don't want to come across as hiding anything, especially your true emotions, because you will look unsure, untrustworthy, and deceptive. Keep your hands out of your pockets. If you have to put them in your pockets, or it's a comfortable stance you prefer, at least keep your thumbs of power out.

Closed palms

I've already mentioned showing your palms makes you appear sincere, open, and trustworthy. When your palms are open you are basically saying, "I'm showing you my hand [as in a game of poker]. I have nothing to hide." Conversely, when you hide your palms it sends the message that you are keeping something to yourself, an emotion or a thought. People who talk with their palms facing inward toward the body (if it's not their baseline) may be feeling insecure, or they may not be telling you the whole truth. If you have baselined someone who normally talks with her palms open and then she suddenly shifts to closing them or facing them inward toward the body, this is a deviation and may be an indicator of deception, or at least lying by omission. As always, look for other tells.

Hand to the head

Hands going to the head (face, neck, hair, top of head) usually indicates high stress and/or deception. You don't want to give an impression that you are uncertain or untrustworthy, so try to avoid touching your face, head, and neck. But you'll know what it means when you see others do it. Following are some examples of the different ways we put our hands to different parts of our head, and their respective meanings.

1. **Hand to mouth.** A hand near the mouth usually means one of what I call the four Ds: disapproval, deep thought, an internal dialogue, or deception. I've already stated that liars will sometimes cover their mouths to hide their deceit (or their "duping delight"). Some people will touch the area above the lip to self-soothe or help them focus. Some will do it as they stare off into space and cogitate or ruminate about something.

Hand to mouth.

This gesture can also indicate skepticism. Brian Wilson did this during much of his interview with Eric Snowdon. You can tell he wasn't buying a word of Snowdon's story! (As a side note, Snowden himself exhibited powerful and confident body language.) In the image above, Chris has his hand to his mouth and his index finger resting on his upper lip. He looks doubtful, even skeptical, about whatever Kelly is telling him, even though Kelly is showing him his palms and subconsciously saying, "I have nothing to hide."

When the hand covers the mouth completely it can indicate surprise, nervousness, shame and embarrassment, or anticipation; it is also often a strong signal of deception. My detainees would often cover their mouths when they lied or leaked duping delight. Unconsciously they were masking what was coming out of their mouths.

Hand to chin.

2. **Hand to chin.** A hand to the chin means "PBC": power, boredom, or contemplation. I'm certain you have seen people resting their chin on their hand, whether in the boardroom, in an audience, during class, in executive profile pictures, or while watching TV. If you look at The Body Language Institute's Website, you'll see Janine Driver's profile picture. Her chin is resting on her hand, and she looks authoritative and powerful. This is another power pose. As Janine says, "Put your hand to your chin to win!" Doing this makes you look powerful and confident. Try this experiment: The next time you are at work pitching a project to your manager, or at a lunch trying to gain a new client contract, or at the dealership trying to sell a used car: when you deliver information, put your hand to your chin. You will appear more trusting and confident. Try it! Steve Jobs, the founder of Apple, was always pictured with his

hand to his chin; it became his iconic pose. In this image Kelly has his hand to his chin as Chris is trying to explain something to him. It looks as though Kelly has already made up his mind and is standing his ground.

A hand placed beneath the mouth, cheek, or chin is a spontaneous and comfortable gesture when people are evaluating, considering, and analyzing. However, it can also indicate fatigue or boredom. When the chin is resting on the hand and the index finger points up to ear, the person is assessing matters; when the index finger rests on the top of the lip, the person is skeptical, distrustful, or potentially deceitful. You can remember what the hand to chin means by remembering the acronym: PBC—power, boredom, or contemplation.

3. **Hand to neck.** If someone is massaging his neck while you talk to him, he is either trying to relax tense muscles or he is stressed out, and the increased blood flow is making his neck itch. The question in your mind should be: Why is he tense or stressed? Some people will rub the back of their neck right before they lie. If you haven't built rapport, or if you have just lost rapport, this person could be saying unconsciously, "You're a pain in my neck." A neck rub can also indicate flirtatious behavior if a woman touches her neck dimple and then her neck while tilting her head and exposing her carotid artery. It's a disarming gesture that says, "I'm open." You will be able to differentiate the two pretty easily.

4. **Head scratch.** If you see someone rubbing or scratching her head, as Vladimir Putin often has been seen doing in photos, it could suggest that she is either in deep thought, confused, or in a state of disbelief. It can also indicate deception, as was the case when Lance Armstrong was seen scratching his head during interviews about his doping, prior to his public admission. The head scratch can also be

an unconscious attempt to draw attention away from the mouth, where a lie is about to come out. If a head scratch is accompanied by a neck scratch, the person could be saying, "I have no idea what I'm saying to you." Of course, it could just be that the person's head itches. If you are pitching your new idea to your boss and he scratches his head, scrunches his nose, and tightens his lips into a thin line, find another idea.

Seven Signs of Uncertainty

1. The shoulder shrug

I love the shoulder shrug because it's such a clear signal; virtually all of the time it indicates uncertainty. But it doesn't always indicate deception. You have to watch the shoulder line pretty carefully, because some shrugs are barely noticeable. The shoulders may rise almost imperceptibly, as little as a breath causes the belly to rise. Sometimes a shoulder shrug is so obvious and extreme, it's clear that the person has given up. Sometimes people do this unconsciously as they commit to something, thereby belying their certainty. A shoulder shrug by itself does not necessarily indicate deception; you have to look for clusters in order to determine deception.

In November 2013, a story broke about a gay waitress, Dayna Morales, who worked at the Asian Gallop Bistro in New Jersey. She posted on Facebook that she served a couple one night and instead of leaving her a tip they left a note saying they didn't agree with her "lifestyle." It went viral. People started donating money to her, I'm not sure why, but she said she was going to donate the money to the Wounded Warrior project. She received about $3,000. A pretty nice gesture, huh? The problem came a week later, when the couple she served that night saw her on the news showing the meal receipt with the note written on it. Realizing it was their receipt, they knew they hadn't written any note on there; they had, however, written in an $18 tip. They contacted the news station and were interviewed. They stated that in no way did they agree with the hateful sentiment of the message; in fact, they considered themselves to be very tolerant of others' beliefs and lifestyles. Plus, the note wasn't even their hand-writing. The news station went back to interview Dayna, saying the couple she accused had come forward and provided their copy of the receipt, which clearly showed an $18 tip but no nasty messages; they also provided a copy of their bank statement, which showed the charge for the meal, including the $18 tip, taken out. When she was asked about how this happened, all Dayna could do was stick to her story and say, "Uh, that's not my handwriting. I don't know. Again—" while she continued to shrug her shoulders and raise her eyebrows. Yes, she showed behavioral congruency by demonstrating uncertain-ty by shrugging her shoulders as she stated, "I don't know," but to me it seemed more like she was saying, "I don't know how I'm gonna get out of this." When the newscaster asked, "Can you see why this cou-ple is upset?" Dayna replied, "I, I guess. I mean, I'm— Sure," shoulder shrugging the entire time. Was she uncertain that they were upset? Surely she must have known that they were upset, and why, but per-haps she was uncertain of being caught. She also used stuttering and stalling techniques, which I'll discuss in the next chapter. Dayna ex-hibited a nice cluster of deceptive tells for us. Not surprisingly, it was later found out that Dayna lied and made the whole thing up. Most of the $3,000 in donations she collected from the random people who were sympathetic to her cause and had fallen victim to her scam, was returned to the donators.

2. Balling up

If you have ever felt vulnerable, sad, depressed, ashamed, or de-feated in any way, you probably tried to make yourself appear smaller. Liars ball up purposefully as a plea for pity. If someone shrugs her shoulders, faces her palms upward, scrunches up her neck, and tucks her chin in, she is most likely trying to make herself appear smaller and more vulnerable. Be careful, though: Sometimes people will ball up right before they strike out in anger. Think of a cobra coiling up before it strikes. If someone is angry and suddenly becomes smaller,

The fig leaf.

you may want to stand back. This is not a sign of uncertainty; this is a sign of rage about to come uncoiled.

3. The fig leaf position

I talked about the three vulnerable areas of the body in Chapter 5: the neck dimple, the stomach, and the groin area. I often see military members and government officials in particular stand with their hands clasped in front of their private parts. I call this the fig leaf stance. Although we think of this as a respectful stance, it is actually a respectful submissive stance. If you want to show respect but also confidence, rather than submissiveness, stand with your hands behind your lower back instead of in the fig leaf position. This sends the signal you are exposing all three of your vulnerable zones because you have no fear. When we feel vulnerable and stripped of power, value, or self-worth, we tend to close up and subconsciously protect our vital, vulnerable areas. In the previous image, Kelly doesn't look confident; he looks vulnerable and self-protective.

Unfortunately, the fig leaf position has become the default pose to signify respect and a businesslike demeanor, but it actually indicates unease and anxiety. For those of you who want to make a good impression to win a new client or look powerful when up for promotion, expose your private parts (not literally!) and put your hands behind your back.

4. Self-preening

When people experience stress they often try to make themselves feel better with self-touch or self-pacifying gestures, also called self-preening. One of my biggest pet peeves, and one of the most common self-touch gestures, occurs when people stand with T-Rex arms, arms bent at the elbows and tucked in close by their sides, when they are address a group of people, whether it be five or 5,000. They still try to "talk" with their hands, but because their elbows are glued to their sides, their hands move around like those of a tyrannosaurus rex. When we stand with our elbows glued to our sides like this, it sends the message (to others and to ourselves) that we feel insecure or unsure of ourselves. Even if we are trying to exude confidence through other means, like lowering our voice, keeping a wide stance, and raising our chin, if we use T-Rex arms, we negate all of our other efforts. When we are relaxed, confident, and comfortable, we stand with our arms hanging down by our sides, on our hips, or with our hands hooked in our pockets, like James Dean. In the following picture Kelly has his arms tucked closely by his sides. He looks unsure of himself, not confident.

T-Rex arms.

Keynote speakers, TED talk presenters, teachers, and everyone else: If you are on a stage, at a podium, or at the front of a boardroom or a classroom, put your arms down! Relax them by your sides. It's perfectly okay to talk with your hands and be animated—in fact, I encourage that—but don't stand there with those useless T-Rex arms; you'll look silly.

I once witnessed a Marine officer in his services alphas, a sharp-looking, olive green uniform, standing in front of a class to give a presentation. He was brushing imaginary lint off the front pockets of his uniform the entire time. When I approached him afterward and mentioned the "lint," he had no idea that he had been doing it. He was self-preening to subconsciously soothe himself and calm his nerves.

5. Stepping back

People often ask me to observe them when they speak in public so I can coach them to be better presenters. When they lose their train of thought or get stumped, they often take a step back. When we feel uncertain we want to create distance between us and what we feel uncertain about. If you are in a conversation with someone—say, in an interview or during a date—and the person you are conversing with takes a step backward, he just put more space between you. It could be that he's uninterested in you, or feels offended for some reason, or is simply unsure of himself. If he is lying, he may be taking a step back to create physical and moral distance between himself and the lie. Just remember the magic word: clusters.

6. The body shift

My company motto is "Move the body, change your mind; read the body, influence people." Liars know this, and will move their bodies to change their minds—meaning, they will change their posture, sit down, stand up, cross their legs, or lift out of a chair to de-stress. I call this the body shift.

There used to be an HBO series titled *Autopsy With Michael Baden*. Dr. Baden is a world-renowned physician and board-certified forensic pathologist. The 10th edition of *Autopsy* featured two cases, one of which was called "The Lady in the Lake." A viewer named Darlene had written to Dr. Baden via the interactive "Ask Dr. Baden" feature on the HBO Website, wanting to know what really happened to her great-aunt, whose body was found in a car submerged in a lake, years after her disappearance. Dr. Baden agreed to take on the case and eventually it became this show (which, by the way, I cannot find anywhere, online or on HBO). This episode contained one of the greatest body-language training videos I have seen, but because of the sensitivities, which I will share in a moment, I think it was pulled off the network and archived for eternity. Baden examined the skeletal remains found in the car to determine the cause of the death. The producers tracked down the man who was married to Darlene's aunt at the time she disappeared years ago. Both Darlene and Daryl, the son of the deceased woman, were interviewed on the show; neither of them trusted or liked the guy that Daryl's mother married (I'll call him Steve because I can't remember his real name). One day, when Daryl was very young, a pre-teen, he came home from school to the motel that his mother owned, and where he lived with his mother and Steve, to find his mother gone. Steve told Daryl she took off, and then he left Daryl at the motel, never to be seen by Daryl again. HBO found Steve living in Florida and asked him if he would agree to be interviewed by HBO (but it was really by undercover police officers) on the death of Daryl's mom in return for monetary compensation. Steve agreed. During the videotaped interview, the cops changed their line of questioning to be slightly accusatory. Steve picked up on this, became visibly nervous, and asked to end the interview prematurely. Steve displayed myriad verbal and nonverbal deceptive tells during the interview—so many, in fact, that my colleagues and I used it at one point as a training video for deception. Steve was blinking uncontrollably and was swallowing hard; he was literally drying out from anxiety. At one point he became so visibly uncomfortable that he actually lifted up out of his chair (a body shift) and turned to look for an escape, the exit door behind him! He was in full fight-or-flight mode. He also was exhibited numerous verbal deceptive tells, such as stalling techniques (answering a question with a question, using pauses and filler words, and so on). The last I read he was still living in Florida. This guy was a textbook liar, and anyone trained in detecting deception would agree.

7. The Pinocchio effect

When Carlo Collodi wrote *The Adventures of Pinocchio* in 1883, I wonder if he knew about the Pinocchio effect. He created this fictional character that was made out of wood but longed to be a real boy, and whose wooden nose grew every time he lied. Did you know that

when we stress or lie (assuming we are everyday liars and not powerful liars), our noses actually grow? Fortunately, or unfortunately,
you can't see it with the naked eye. When someone is stressed out,
the tissue in the nose becomes engorged with blood, making it swell
ever so slightly and itch. So when you see nervous people swiping at
their noses, it's because it's itching and, yes, growing like Pinocchio's.
During Bill Clinton's grand jury testimony regarding his denied affair with Monica Lewinsky, he swiped at his nose numerous times
and even hid his nose in his hands. Scratching the nose is an almost
certain indicator of stress. Whether it's also an indicator of deception
will be more apparent when you add the next batch of weapons to
your lie-detecting arsenal.

10

E Is for Extract the Truth: Verbal Tells

My 10-year-old niece Christine said to me, "Auntie Lena! You are not going to believe this, but, um, I can hold my breath for five minutes!" I replied, "Really?" She giggled and said, "Well, almost! Come watch me and count!" Now, I know she can't hold her breath for five minutes; if she could, she'd be in the *Guinness Book of World Records*. But if she had said, "Auntie Lena! You are not going to believe this, but, um, I got an A in math on my report card!" I still wouldn't have believed her, for two reasons: first, she *hedged* her statement by indirectly telling me not to believe her; and second, she paused and used a filler word ("um"). Both of these clues together in one sentence tell me that whatever is coming out of her mouth next will pretty much be an embellishment at best, and a lie at worst. (Now, this clue about hedging is not an absolute; you have to baseline someone's customary way of speaking, just as you have to baseline body language.)

In the Jodi Arias interrogation video I mentioned in Chapter 5, Jodi is left alone in the interrogation room, handcuffed behind her back and sitting in a chair with her head on the table. After a minute or so she decides to sit on the floor, bend over, and forcefully flip her head and hair back. A woman enters and asks her to sit in the chair. She sits back in the chair and puts her head back on the table. A detective enters to talk to her and reads her rights. At one point she asks the detective, "Um, this is a really trivial question, and it's going to reveal how shallow I am, but before they book me, can I clean myself up a little bit?" You said it, Jodi, not us: You are indeed shallow for wanting to make yourself look good before they book you for brutally slaying your boyfriend. If we break apart this sentence, you will see three verbal "hot spots" or tells: first, she uses a filler word, which is essentially a spoken pause to give the mind time to think of what to say next; second, she uses the word "really," which is sometimes used by people to emphasize their perceived truthfulness and reinforce their lie; and third, she uses the word "but," which is commonly used to hedge a statement. She likely knows that asking this will make her look bad, so she uses "really" to minimize the trivial and shallow nature of the request (wanting to look good). When people use the word "but," it is usually meant to minimize, soften, or weaken the value or significance of what is about to be said. Jodi is trying to weaken or minimize the full import of being concerned about cleaning herself up. She also does this by sounding demure and sincere, in hopes the detective will focus on that instead of the fact she is being booked for murdering her ex-boyfriend. I'll talk more about hedging statements later on.

This chapter focuses on verbal (both spoken and written) deceptive tells. We are going to dissect sentences to see what the words really mean in context. Words are important! People choose to use specific words, both consciously and unconsciously, for a reason. We will conduct *statement analysis*, a term coined by Mark McClish, a retired deputy United States marshal with 26 years of federal law enforcement experience. He developed this method to determine whether a person is lying or telling the truth by analyzing the subject's language.

I am also going to teach you four steps I follow to extract the truth from deceitful people. You will learn how to listen attentively and *timeline* events of a story so you can fill in the missing information (usually out of lying by omission). I will teach you 10 common verbal deceptive tells (deviations in verbal language). You will learn how to make people feel good about themselves by boosting their pride and ego. And you will learn how to use questioning techniques to extract the truth *while maintaining rapport*. This is the crux of this book, because not only do I want you to be able to get rid of deception from your life, but I want you to know the truth, too. Because you deserve it.

You may wonder why I call it truth extraction (which sounds a lot like tooth extraction). There is a reason. Do you remember the Milton Bradley game Operation, the one in which you had those metal tweezers to extract silly items from a male patient? If you weren't careful extracting the butterfly from his stomach, or the funny bone from his elbow, your tweezers would hit the metal sides, and a loud buzzer would go off while his red nose lit up. When you are extracting the truth from someone, you have to be just as careful. You don't want to alert the person to what you are trying to do. If you are interrogating or interviewing someone who is doing his best to resist your techniques and stick to a cover story, truth extraction becomes a skillful conversation in which you need to conceal your true intentions and objectives while getting him to confess to the truth. You can do this by carefully asking questions, using elicitation techniques, and controlling the conversation. It's about making sure you don't make his buzzer go off (tip him off) by making him uncomfortable, guilty, nervous, or worried about what he just told you or what you are asking. If you ask poor questions or the wrong questions, you will not get the information you want. Using bad questioning techniques will only frustrate the two of you. If you are both frustrated and emotional, you will most likely lose rapport with that person. And if you lose rapport, you may never get the truth. He may even shut down the conversation entirely. If this happens, my advice is get someone else to question him if you can. At that point, you have probably lost your credibility, so no matter how sincere and convincing you try to be to bring him back around, you probably won't succeed.

As a former interrogator, I felt that questioning required more skill and tact than any other step in the interrogation process. Building rapport was easy, using our approach techniques was easy, but properly asking questions, fully exploiting topics, and controlling conversations, all while you are trying to maintain rapport and weave in various approaches, was tough. I am going to teach you questioning skills that will never fail you, if used properly.

Here are my four steps for extracting the truth:

1. Timeline events.
2. Listen for verbal hot spots.
3. Use "pride and ego up."
4. Ask good questions.

Step 1: Timeline Events

A sure way to get detailed information, leaving no stone unturned, and no topic unexploited, is to use a technique I call *timelining*. Timelining is a super effective way to catch someone in a lie—so effective, in fact, that I used this technique in all my interrogations to gather the details of a story that my detainees *wanted* to tell, according to a time line. I italicize *wanted* because most detainees wanted to lie to me; they wanted to tell me a fabricated story—we called them "cover stories"—about why they were in Afghanistan; it was their safe story. They knew how to create a story with just enough details so it would appear to be truthful, but not so many that they couldn't remember any of them. Their story contained small bits of truthful information that they were willing and ready to share, mixed in with their overall cover story. They had to be careful about how many details they made up, because the more they invented, the more they would have to remember, and remembering details that aren't true is really difficult to do; in fact, most of the time it's virtually impossible. Their stories were vague for that very reason. I like to say that details are the death of a lie, because if you fail to give any details, that is an indication that you are lying and don't want to have to remember false details. Conversely, if you do give me details but they are lies, I'll catch you tripping up on those fabricated details when I question you later. So either way, exposing and exploiting details will expose your lie.

Did you know that liars can't remember a lie backward? Timelining detainees' stories allowed me to see those stories in reverse, something they hadn't foreseen or practiced for. So when I asked one to tell me again why he went to Afghanistan, this time I had him start from the time he arrived at GTMO, going back in time to the very first event that started his original story. Every single one of them who told me a cover story, a fabricated story (and that was most of them), would mess up the details of their story, leave out information, or add more facts. Nothing ever matched up with my notes from the original version. Remember that the next time someone tells you a story that seems off; ask her to tell you it again, but in reverse. If she can't, the story probably wasn't true to begin with. I say probably, because if you are like me and can't remember dates and times (whether you are going forward or backward), you'll never be able to do this, even if you are telling the truth! If you decide to use this technique, you'd better be a good listener, because if you can't retain the details to question the person on later, you will have already failed.

As I listened and took notes my goal was to drill down and get every minute detail so I could find all the verbal hot spots. Timelining helped me collect every detail that I needed to break apart a cover story. As an interrogator you have a hundred things going on in your mind at once, from running approach techniques, building rapport, working with an interpreter, tag-teaming with individuals from law enforcement agencies, using specialized equipment, taking copious notes while listening attentively to every word uttered, and watching assiduously every gesture made. You are doing 10 things at once all the time, and it is exhausting. So in order for me to ensure I didn't miss any details of a story, I timelined it so I could tear it apart at my own pace.

Doing this also helped in building rapport. I never wanted to start off being accusatory, because the detainees never would have wanted to talk to me. So I would be super nice and respectful, and listen to their stories, even if it was one of the ridiculous cover stories *du jour* that circulated among the detainee population. One detainee would come up with the perfect cover story as to why he went to Afghanistan; he would then share that story with the other detainees, thinking they could all use it. We would have 50 detainees all telling us they went to Afghanistan to find a bride. How could they not see how absurd that was? I would say, "That's lovely! Did you find one?" None of them ever said that they had, or answered, "No, but I found the Taliban!" I took the time to listen to their cover stories so I could build rapport with them and eventually get the *real* stories.

The importance of verb tense

When liars create a story that isn't true, they are creating it in the present tense, because it never happened. Therefore, it is not recalled information. A verbal hot spot to look out for is abrupt changes in verb tense. Liars have a hard enough time remembering the details of a lie, so when they are in the act of spinning their story, they will often mix up verb tenses. They try to tell the lie in the past tense, as something that already happened, but because it never happened, you will often see the present tense popping up.

Viewing a story as a series of events in chronological order will allow you to see the gaps in the time line (that is, the gaps in the liar's story). Once you identify chunks of missing time and information, you can then use effective questioning techniques to probe the subject for missing information. Once you have completely filled in the time line, you can fully exploit each event for details. This is where you will find the lies. After thoroughly questioning the subject about the entire time line, you can ask him to tell you the story in reverse, a proven technique to catch a liar. Why? Because liars can't remember a lie backward. Why? Because they made the story up in the present tense, in chronological order, they never gave a thought to how the lie would have happened in reverse. They may remember certain key events, but they will be out of sequence; then they will forget details and get frustrated, flustered, and defensive. Once a liar starts to fall apart, you can start to chisel away at his will to resist telling the truth.

Let's look at Larry King's live interview with Patsy and John Ramsey in 2000 after their daughter, Jon-Benet, was found murdered in their home. I have transcribed the conversation, but I encourage you to Google the interview or watch it on YouTube so that you can see the body language and facial expressions, too.

(Larry King = LK, John Ramsey = JR, Patsy Ramsey = PR)

LK: "Let's go back to that night. It's December 26, the day after Christmas, right? That's when this occurred."

JR: "Uh huh."

LK: "You've spent part of Christmas Day at your friend's house. Give us a little history. You were in what business in Boulder?"

JR: "We were in the computer business, distribution business. We sold computer products to resellers who then sold them to users."

LK: "Very successful, right?"

JR: "It was, uh, reasonably successful."

LK: "So you have two children?"

JR: "Yeah." [*looks at Patsy*]

PR: "Two children."

LR: "You lost a daughter previously in a previous marriage, right?"

JR: "My oldest daughter, Beth, was killed in an automobile accident in Chicago in 1992."

LK: "You lost two daughters."

JR: "Two daughters. My oldest and my youngest."

LK: "What happened that day?"

JR: "December...twenty...sixth?"

LK: "Sixth."

JR: [*sighs*] "We were planning to leave for, uh, Charlevoix, which is...we have, uh, a summer cottage up there. Did have... uh...we were gonna rendezvous with our kids for uh, uh, first ever family Christmas, all together in Michigan. We were to leave early that morning, uh...um, fly to Michigan."

[*Author' note: Notice all the filler words and the sigh, signs of stress and trying to think about what to say next.*]

LK: "Morning after Christmas."

JR: "Morning after."

LK: "What happened that night? What's the first thing you remember, Patsy?"

PR: "The first thing I remember is...waking up, getting dressed hurriedly, going downstairs, and, uh, putting a few things together to pack to take on the plane."

LK: "This is about what time?"

PR: "It's early morning, before daylight."

LK: [*to John Ramsey*] "You're up?"

JR and PR: [*together*] "Uh huh."

LK: "Then what happened?"

PR: "Then I, I [*stutters*] go down the spiral staircase [*making spiral motion with her hands*] and...there on one of the rungs of the stair is a three-page ransom note."

[*Author's note: The number three is, oddly, widely used by liars. In fact, it's called the* liar's number. *Perhaps it's because people can more easily remember chunks of information in threes. Stuttering is also a sign of stress. But the most significant word in their statement so far is—can you guess? It's the word "is." Remember what I told you about liars creating a story, a lie, in present tense, and so they tell the story in present tense even though it supposedly happened in the past? Patsy should have said "was a three-page ransom note." She switched from past tense to present tense at the most significant juncture in the*] *story, the appearance of the ransom note. This is a verbal hot spot.)*

LK: "And no one has entered the house, door isn't open, you read the note..."

PR: "I don't know that." [*Patsy is smiling.*]

LK: "What did you do?"

PR: [*still smiling*] "Well. I hardly even read it, you know, and didn't take long to understand [*pause*] what [*pause*] was happening, and I ran back up stairs and pushed open her bedroom door and she was gone."

[*Author's note: Why is Patsy smiling? Duping delight, perhaps?*]

Her story, which I believe is completely fabricated because of all the hot spots I pointed out, is told on a time line, but did you see how the timeline is not right? Patsy claims she went downstairs to pack a few things before she found the three page ransom note. Did she walk right by it the first time? Or did she put it on the rung of the stair the second time? I don't know what their house looked like, but if there was more than one set of stairs, perhaps she went down a different staircase earlier. This is definitely a hot spot that the technique of timelining will help clarify. If I were Larry King I would have asked what time she did all of these things: got up in the morning, got dressed, went downstairs to pack a few things, found the three-page ransom note, opened the door to her daughter's bedroom. Even if she gave times as an approximation, you would still have a rough time line. To show you how I use this technique in interrogations, I'll create some answers for an imaginary timelining dialogue:

LS: "Patsy, what time did you get up the morning of December 26?"

PS: It's early morning, before the sun is up."

LS: "About what time did you get up?" [*I ask her again because she didn't answer my question.*]

PS: "It's about 5:00 a.m."

LS: "What time did you get dressed?"

PS: "I immediately got dressed."

LS: "What time did you get dressed?" [*another repeat question*]

PS: "Well, I washed up and got dressed by 5:15, I guess."

LS: "What time did you go downstairs to pack a few things?"

PS: "At 5:15 I went downstairs to pack a few things."

LS: "What time did you go down the spiral staircase and find the three-page ransom note?"

Now I don't know what she would have said next; would she have tried to cover up the fact that she told us she went downstairs twice and didn't see the ransom note the first time? Or would she claim that she went down a different staircase earlier, came back up, and then went down the spiral staircase? I don't know. But can do you see how timelining can punch holes in a fabricated story? The other great thing about timelining a lie is the fact that you can use the times given to cross-reference and fact-check the story. If Patsy's story is true, those times shouldn't deviate much, if at all. If this story is a lie, she won't remember the details of times, and she will mix them up *and* confuse the order of events. I encourage you to practice time-lining on people you think are being deceptive, whether it is your daughter claiming the cigarettes you found in her coat pocket weren't hers, or your employee telling you he had no idea how that $200 in cash was stolen from the cash register.

Two important caveats: When you are timelining, be very careful not to sound as though you were interrogating the person with robotic questions, because he or she will get defensive and you will lose rapport. You need to maintain rapport with your subjects while questioning them so they *want* to stay in the conversation. You also don't want to attack them or accuse them of wrongdoing. People confess to things when they feel comfortable doing so, when they have rapport with their questioner, when the questioner makes them feel like it's okay or understandable that they did what they did. I'll discuss this technique further in the third step, use pride and ego up. To the interrogators, investigators, and interviewers reading this book: If you don't already do it, start timelining; it will save you time and frustration.

Step 2: Listen for Verbal Hot Spots

People use the words they do for a reason; thus, they are just as important as reading body language when it comes to detecting deception. Here are 11 verbal hot spots (including changing verb tense) that can indicate deception. I write "can" because you already know my rule of three: baseline, look for clusters of tells, and be aware of the context in which the information is being delivered.

1. Pronoun use

Liars tend to avoid using the words "I" and "my." This helps to distance themselves from the lie. Most people are raised to be honest, and generally speaking, people don't like to lie. When they do, they want to remove themselves from the dishonest act. It also allows liars to not have to definitive answer. When Congressman Anthony Weiner first spoke out regarding the photo on his Twitter account, he refused to say whether or not the picture was of him. All he kept saying was that his account had been hacked. When a reporter asked, "Can you tell me definitively, is that a photograph of you?" Weiner responded, "We are trying to find out the—where that photograph came from." A few hot spots stand out here. First, he was asked a yes-or-no question that he would not answer with a yes or a no. Second, who is "we"? Why couldn't he have just said, "I'm trying to find out where it came from"? Because he was lying and wanted to remove himself from the lie. He later went on to say, "I said, let's try to figure out who, how, what this—how this prank went down, how we make sure it doesn't happen again." Again, why is he using the first person plural? His stuttering and hesitating was another hot spot. Of course we now know for a fact that he was lying. Later, when he finally came clean and apologized publicly, he was no longer removing or distancing himself. The "we" became "I": "I have made terrible mistakes, I've hurt the people I care about the most, and I'm deeply sorry." Pronoun usage can tell us a lot about whether someone is being deceptive.

Sometime you'll hear pronoun usage switch. For example, back in November 2001, the Northern Alliance, under the control of General Dostum and aided by other countries, including the United States, captured members of the Taliban and al Qaeda, and held them at Qala-i-Jangi Fortress in Mazar-i-Sharif, Afghanistan, while trying to peacefully reason with the Taliban commander. Reason didn't work, and what ensued was a three-day massacre. Out of hundreds of Taliban, al Qaeda, and foreign fighters, 86 survived, one of whom was John Walker Lindh, known as the American Taliban. When CNN interviewed him, he went from saying *we* [the Taliban] were fighting for a cause," to saying (about 10 minutes later) "it was one of *them* [the Taliban] who threw the grenade." His shift from first personal plural, where he associated himself with the Taliban, to third person plural, where he distances himself from them, is a verbal hot spot or deviation. Just as with all other verbal tells, you have to listen carefully to pick up on these kinds of pronoun changes and shifts.

2. Verb tense changes

I've already illustrated how Patsy Ramsey mixed up her verb tenses in her timeline. Remember: When we tell a lie, we rehearse it in the present tense, so we forget to tell it in the past tense.

3. Non-contracted denials

People who "protest too loudly"—liars who are overly determined in their denial—often resort to formal language. Liars do not like to use contractions because they are trying to emphasize their lie making it appear believable by breaking apart contractions (remember that liars convince, while truthful people convey): "I *did not* do that," "that *is not* true," "we *would not* say that." Both Bill Clinton and Anthony Weiner were famous for their non-contracted denials. Witness Clinton's famous words: "I did not have sexual relations with that woman, Ms. Lewinski. I never told anybody to lie, not a single time, never." I'll discuss this statement again later because there are actually two more verbal hot spots. And Anthony Weiner: "The answer is I did not send that [*pause*] tweet." Be on the alert if you hear someone suddenly use non-contracted denials; he's trying to emphasize what he is saying for some reason. It doesn't always mean someone is being deceptive, of course; so as always, use my rule of three for greater certainty.

4. Can't simply say yes or no

Anthony Weiner and Bill Clinton had this unfortunate problem, as well. The golden rule to follow is that if you are asking a yes-or-no question, you should get a yes or a no in response within three tries. If not, that person is hiding something. Sometimes you will get what I call substitute words. Substitute words for *yes* include *absolutely, of course, definitely,* and *always.* Notice that none of these words is actually *yes.* Substitute words for *no* include *of course not, not ever, certainly not,* and *never* (which I'll talk about next by itself), none of which is a substitute for *no.* As an interrogator I considered yes-or-no questions bad questions because they don't elicit a narrative response, and hence are unlikely to yield new information. However, if they are used properly, and inserted to test for truthfulness, they can be very useful indeed. Asking a yes-or-no question is like asking someone what's the fifth word in the "Star Spangled Banner" is: It's a quick and easy baseline.

Although the word "never" is a negative word, it is not a replacement for no. It is easier for someone to be evasively dishonest by using the word *never* than it is to directly tell a lie by saying no. Answering with *never* can sometimes fool the interviewer. That said, this doesn't automatically mean a person is being deceptive. There are perfectly correct and legitimate ways to use the word. For example, if I said, "I have never been skydiving," it would be a truthful statement. However, using *never* as a substitute for *no* can be an indication of deception when it's being used to avoid giving a direct "no." Remember to baseline. I use the word "never" all the time; I even use it to mean *no* when I'm being truthful.

Let's look at Lance Armstrong again when he appeared on Sports News Television in 2005, denying, under oath, his use of steroids to win the Tour de France. Here is part of the transcribed dialogue from Armstrong's sworn deposition. (You can also view the entire thing on YouTube: *www.youtube.com/watch?v=klz86uQMrVg*.)

> Interviewer: "Just want to make sure: it's not that you don't re-member that the Indiana hospital room incident occurred; it, it affirmatively did not take place."
>
> LA: "I know it did not. How could it have taken place when I've never taken performance-enhancing drugs? Look, how could that have happened?"
>
> Interviewer: "That was my point. You're not, it's not just sim-ply that you don't recall—"
>
> LA: "How many times do I have to say it?"
>
> Interviewer: "I'm just trying to make sure your testimony is clear."
>
> LA: "Well, if it can't be any clearer than I've never taken drugs, then incidents like that could never have happened."
>
> Interviewer: "Okay."
>
> LA: "How clear is that?"
>
> Interviewer: "Okay, I think it's clear."

If you watch this video you will also see Lance use the "knife hand" gesture, as though he were chopping the air with the side of his hand, to make a point. You can hear him getting defensive and belligerent. Lance was what we call a *severe convincer*; he would get aggressive, accusatory, and confrontational when anyone dared ques-tion him about his use of performance-enhancing drugs.

5. Answering a question with a question

If you ask someone, "Where were you last night?" and she responds with another question, such as, "Why do you want to know where I was last night?" this is almost always an indicator of deception. If she has nothing to hide, she would have just answered your question. People with nothing to hide, don't hide! It's not a question of her not hearing your question, since she asked one in response. This is simply a stalling technique to buy time to think of what to say. The only other reason to answer a question with a question would be if the person being asked felt that the person asking didn't trust them, and that meant more to them than answering the question. So if you ask your significant other a pointed question, and he replies with a question, he could simply be upset that you doubted him enough to even ask, and wants to find out why before he answers. Most often, though, it's used as a stalling technique.

6. Repeating the question

This is a subset of the previous hot spot. Unless you're talking to someone who doesn't speak your language and is trying to make sure he understands the question, he is stalling and buying himself some time to answer. It doesn't necessarily mean he's about to lie, but it does mean he felt he needed that extra second to think of how to respond. I actually know people who do this all the time as their baseline; my father is one of them. Whether he truly cannot hear me (his hearing is not as sharp as it once was) or he just isn't paying attention (because he's more interested in his British comedy TV shows), whenever I ask him a question, he often repeats it back to me. So be sure to baseline.

7. Filler words

Words such as *um, uh,* and *ah* are filler words or stall words used to give the mind time to think of what to say next. I also like to call them *pet words,* because when people are nervous they tend to use their favorite filler words over and over again, especially when they are speaking in public. They use these words as pacifiers, but just as pacifying body gestures do, they only make them look nervous, unsure, and deceptive. If you know or have been told you use filler words when you speak, break the habit now. Start practicing your speeches in the car, in the shower, wherever you can be alone, and start consciously avoiding them. Only practice will make you more confident; soon you won't be using them. Let's look once again at this transcribed dialogue between the Ramsey's and Larry King to see stalling techniques in action and hear how unsure of themselves it makes people sound:

LK: "Okay, police are there, friends come over. What happened to Burke? Does he stay asleep? Or do you wake him up and send it? What happens to Burke?

JR: "Burke, uh, was in bed, uh... [*pause/stutter*] We, uh, got him up, uh, don't remember what time, but we [*pause*] had him go to a friend's house. Uh, I told him his sister was missing, uh..."

LK: "Told him the truth."

JR: "Told him the truth. We didn't [*pauses, then shakes head no as he shrugs his shoulders*] try to make it [*pause*] as easy on him as we could, but he cried immediately, so he knew something seriously was wrong, uh, and he went to a friend's house."

The total conversation time is 43 seconds. John Ramsey uses "uh" seven times in 43 seconds, and he stutters or pauses at length four times. Why is he concentrating so hard on what to say? In my opinion, it seems as though he were trying to remember a fabricated lie of what he and his wife were saying happened that day, while perhaps seeing in his mind what *really* happened. But this is only my opinion. Certainly, neither one has been convicted of any crime, and even suspects are considered innocent until proven guilty.

8. Hedging statements

Hedging a statement—prefacing a statement with another statement in order to be deceptive—is not used to show caution, but rather to intentionally create vagueness that obscures the facts in and details of another statement. It softens what's about to come next. Such statements come across as polite and modest, so the listener's guard is down, along with his or her awareness. Such statements can be used as smokescreens that hide or take the focus off what comes after, which is usually the important piece of information, and usually where the deception is embedded. Liars love to hedge their statements because it allows them to avoid responsibility and evade the truth. It's similar to the way an illusionist gets the audience to focus on one thing so they can't see the means or method of the illusion. Liars desperately want you to focus on the hedged statement, so when you hear one, it should be a signal to pay close attention to what comes *after* it.

I want to talk briefly about the experience of being smokescreened. In the interrogation world we call it "being taken down the rabbit hole." When my detainees wanted to take me down the rabbit hole—that is, take my focus off pertinent topics and on to a non-pertinent one—they would be very nice and cooperative and would want to talk up a storm, but only about what they wanted to talk about. They thought by being cooperative and friendly, they would be able to hide the fact they were talking about nothing of importance, nothing that had any intelligence value. They would tell me elaborate stories that, in the words of Shakespeare, were "much ado about nothing." Some junior interrogators would let the detainees ramble on and on for hours, for fear of losing rapport and having him shut down if they stopped the smokescreen story. I would take the interrogator out and give him a pep talk to get back in the booth and put a stop to the nonsense. The detainee was doing nothing but wasting the interrogator's time until he was allowed to go back to his cell. We didn't have the luxury of time, especially when we needed to get information to the soldiers on the battlefield and the people at the agencies. Don't let yourself be taken down the rabbit hole. People will try desperately to bring you there if they are trying to hide information.

Have you ever tried to confront your significant other about why he came home so late, only to have him go off on a story/tangent that had nothing do with why he came home late or where he had been? Or worse, have him turn the conversation back around on you by saying how hurt he was that you didn't trust him? Have you ever confronted your child about the bad progress report she received, only to hear her complain about how the teacher has a vendetta against her and how mean he is to her? If so, you've been smokescreened. People will create a smokescreen, just like the giant puff of smoke that appears to hide what the magician is really doing, to steer you away from the subject they want to avoid. Who wants to say, "Darling, I got this gorgeous new winter coat. It was way too much money—$1,000—but I had to have it!" None of us, right? So we may say instead, "Darling, I finally found a winter coat—you know how I have been looking for one for ages? I'll be able to wear it to your company's Christmas party now! I didn't have a nice one I could wear when I have to dress up, and I want to look good for you. It was even on sale!" That's a lot of extraneous information, just to tell your husband that you bought a new coat. That extra fluff about the Christmas party and looking good for him, means you are trying to smokescreen him by making him feel good and happy for you, and prevent him from coming back and asking, "How much was the coat?" thus forcing you to admit that you dropped a significant amount of cash on it. I'm pretty sure I've done this, but with shoes.

I am going to use another transcription from the Jodi Arias interview, so you can see her smokescreen while she tells the story about how Travis was murdered, a story that later proved to be a lie. The video is just full of juicy deceptive tells! Jodi is in the midst of telling the story (read: lie) about what happened the day her ex-boyfriend Travis Alexander was brutally murdered:

> JA: "We woke up around one, um, I'd say, o'clock in the afternoon. When we woke up we had sex twice, once in his bed and once in his office downstairs."
>
> [*Commentary: "And then, just like old times, they pulled out the camera."*]

JA: "We decided to do another photo shoot, um, where we were going to just get him in the shower, but these were waist up shots—you know, tasteful shots."

Interviewer: "He was in the shower?"

JA: "He was in the shower. Hm, the shower was on, it looked really cool because the way the water was frozen in the image."

[*Author's note: In this last statement her rate of speech quickens. She is smokescreening the interviewer by focusing on how cool the water looked, frozen in time, in her photography. She is taking the focus off the fact that Travis was found shot and stabbed 27 times, and on to the shower water looking "cool" in her picture. She is painting a picture of an image that she wants the interviewer to have of them being romantic, flirty, happy, and artistic, rather than her stabbing and shooting Travis in a crazy jealous rage and leaving his dead body slumped in the shower. A smokescreen tells us, "Don't focus on that, focus on this."*]

The but syndrome hedge

I've already talked about how Jodi Arias used the word *but* when she said, "Um, this is a really trivial question, and it's going to reveal how shallow I am, but..." to downplay the significance of being concerned about freshening up before she was booked for murder. Have you ever heard someone start telling you story by saying, "I know this sounds crazy, but..." or "You're not going to believe this, but..."? I am sure you have. Did the story seem crazy and unbelievable? It probably was. This person could have been telling you, subconsciously, that the story truly was crazy and you shouldn't believe it! Ask yourself why someone would need to tell you that you are not going to believe what they are about to say. Remember that most people don't like to lie, so perhaps this was a way for this person to tell you that he was going to lie to you, or at least be dishonest in some way. In other words, it was a circuitous, noncommittal way of being—honest! Some people use these two particular hedges all the time when they go to tell a story so it may be their normal behavior, but if their stories are always embellished then it's probably a deceptive tell. However, remember you must baseline people first before you can say this is a deceptive tell.

The oath hedge

"I swear to God I am telling you the truth," "As God is my witness," "I swear on my mother's/father's grave." These are all oaths people use when they want to be taken seriously. Both truthful and deceptive people use them, so be sure to baseline. Deceptive individuals will try to give interviewers as little useful information as possible, while doing their best to convince interviewers that what little they say is true. They will often use mild oaths to try to make their statements sound more convincing. Deceptive people are more likely than truthful people to sprinkle their statements with expressions such as "I swear," "on my honor," and "cross my heart." This verbal hot spot falls under the "convince, not convey" category. Remember: Liars want to convince us of the lie, whereas truthful people convey their true story. They do need feel the need to convince anyone of anything by backing their statements with empty oaths, because they are more confident that the facts will prove the veracity of their statements.

"Actually"

I love this word, because just as a shoulder shrug means uncertainty 100 percent of the time, this word means there is another thought 100 percent of the time. If you said to me, "Actually, I'm a financial advisor," my first instinct is to wonder, *What else are you?* If you truly were a financial advisor, you would have just said so: "I'm a financial advisor," but the fact that you felt the need to hedge the statement with *actually* tells one of several things: either you just became one and were something else; you want to become one but aren't yet (maybe you are still in school); you were one but now have moved on to something else; or you are something else and decided to just tell me you are a financial advisor. Even though the word "actually" always means there is another thought or idea or fact, it does not always mean it is deception.

9. Distancing language

For this, let's look at Clinton's famous words: "I did not have sexual relations with that woman, Ms. Lewinski. I never told anybody to lie, not a single time, never." This statement is littered with verbal deception, but I bet he thought he was making himself look pretty confident and poised at the time. You can see his use of a non-contracted denial ("did not"), his use of the word "never" to reinforce his lie, and his clever use of distancing language to remove himself from the action. Why is Monica Lewinsky, the woman he clearly knew, suddenly "that woman," a stranger? Because Bill wanted us to think that she was a stranger to him, and so he couldn't have had an affair with her. But Bill did a poor job of that. People will distance themselves from persons, places, and things by not using names, titles, or designations. People will distance themselves from events or actions by using vague terminology. In my world as an Intelligence professional, I often couldn't say what I was doing, so I would call it "work" or "training."

10. Softening language

People will soften the harshness or reality of the truth through the use of noncommittal or softening language. Here are some examples of softening language, with my comments after each:

Q: "Where were you when she was murdered?"

A: "I was at home when she passed."

Passed is a softer way of saying *died*, which is in turn much softer than *murdered*. It also removes any possibility of any blame since there was no murder.

Q: "Did you abort her unborn child?"

A: "Her pregnancy was terminated because of a miscarriage."

Again, *abort* is a pretty harsh word with really ugly images; *terminated* is a much softer, more clinical statement. Also note the use of the passive voice, another way to create distance between the actor and the action.

Q: "How many times did you stab your ex-boyfriend?"

A: "I hit him three times before I could get away."

Hitting is not stabbing, plain and simple. The interrogator here would have to try to get this individual to admit to stabbing by forcing her to use that word. Sometimes it's just a matter of getting the person to admit it to him- or herself. People may admit to a crime in a nominal sense, but they may not have consciously taken responsibility for the severity of it yet, so they still talk about it using softening language.

During Chris Cuomo's CNN interview with Amanda Knox (watch it on YouTube: *www.youtube.com/watch?v=J_NQKBZBsyo*), Amanda Knox continued to defend herself against accusations that she murdered Meredith Kercher:

AK: "I—[pause]—I did not kill my friend. I did not wield a knife."

The word "wield" is a great example of softening language. Wielding sounds a lot less harsh than "grasp," "grab," "clutch," "clench," or even "hold." What do you picture when you imagine someone wielding a knife versus clenching or grabbing one? I bet there is a difference, and I bet you see someone clenching as more apt to use a knife in a murder. Later in the interview she stated:

AK: "If I were there, I would have traces of Meredith's—[pause]—broken body on me."

Amanda again uses softening language by referring to Meredith's body as "broken." This is odd verbiage to use about her friend's body that had actually been brutally stabbed and cut open.

11. Text bridges

Picture the Golden Gate Bridge in your mind. Now think of a statement such as "I went to the movies" on the Marin County side, and the statement "I came home" on the San Francisco side. Then picture the words "and then" on the bridge. So the entire statement put together would read "I went to the movies and then I came home." The phrase "and then" is a text bridge; it is tying bits of information together while glossing over *what else* might have happened in between those two events. It implies a linear, exhaustive chronological narrative when it is anything but. I've already stated that lying by omission is the preferred way that most of us lie, because we don't have to actually tell a lie; we just have to keep it quiet. Liars will often tell the truth right up to the point where they want to conceal information; then, they skip over the withheld information and tell the truth again. When you hear a text bridge, you should ask yourself what else is on the bridge that is not being mentioned. What does the "and then" cover up? Mark McClish, the creator of statement analysis, states that "a text bridge is a word or phrase that allows a person to transition from one thought to another" (source: *www.all-about-body-language.com/mark-mcclish.html*) while leaving out a thought. Other text bridges include the following words and phrases: *after, afterward, later on, at that point, following, finally, next,* and *the next thing.* You will often hear people say "and the next thing I knew...," which just tells you there is a gap in the information. It doesn't necessarily mean that they are being deceptive and are aware of the information they are purposely skipping over. It may be that they truly don't know what happened during that time. For example, I almost drowned when I was about 12 years old. I was in the rough ocean waters on Misquamicut Beach, Rhode Island. I was pretty small when I was a pre-teen, much smaller than everyone else in my age group at that time. I grew up in the ocean, and my dad made sure all of us kids knew how to swim early on. One day I took off for the beach, along with my cousins who were visiting from Connecticut. I was by myself in the ocean, having fun in the big waves, until this one monster wave came and changed me forever. It was so huge that I couldn't ride over it, so I tried to turn around and run out but the surf was so strong, and I was so small, it just sucked me back in. I didn't know how to dive under the wave to escape it. I'll never forget looking up at this wall of water and seeing it crashing down right on top of me. I was pummeled into the ocean floor and tossed around in the surf for what seemed like an eternity. I told myself, *Relax and let it wash you to shore.* I struck out with my arms and legs to see if I could reach the floor or air. Nothing. I opened my eyes to see if I could see where the light was coming from and which way was up. Still nothing. I couldn't hold my breath any longer. Finally I told myself, *You are going to take a breath under water and drown.* I took a deep intake of breath and *the next thing I remember* was waking up face down in the sand with a crowd of people around me. See? I used a text bridge, but to this day I don't know what happened in that period of time between when I took the breath and when I woke up coughing on the shore. To this day I hyperventilate a little bit when I'm in the ocean, but I won't let it keep me out of it!

Let's see how Jodi Arias used text bridges in another statement from her interview:

JA: "I heard, um, a really loud, um, pop, and **the next thing I remember** I was lying next to the bathtub, and Travis was, um, was screaming."

In addition to all those filler words, she cleverly uses a text bridge to tell the reporter, "I don't know what happened in that chunk of time between when I heard a pop and when I came to, finding Travis badly wounded and seeing two intruders in the bathroom." She implies that she was hit in the head, but never comes right out and says that.

So there are the 11 verbal hot spots that can indicate deception, whether you are listening to someone tell a story or you are reading a confession. Here is a series of questions and answers that illustrate clusters of verbal hot spots. Each response contains more than one verbal hot spot, which I will explain and then show you how to deal with them and extract the truth.

Question: "Did you sell drugs to teenagers?" (This is a yes-or-no question that demands a yes or a no in response.)

Response #1: "I would never do that!"

Remember: Never is not a substitute for no. A good response question would be, "You say you would (conditional future tense) never do that, but have you (past tense) sold drugs to teenagers?" Ask the question again, because the subject did not answer it the first time. Again, look for a yes or a no. The fact that the subject is saying he "would never" in the future does not tell me that he didn't in the past. A narrative response in the past tense would be something like "I didn't sell drugs to teenagers" or "I have never sold drugs to teenagers." You are probably thinking, *Wait, he said* never, *and that's a verbal hot spot!* Yes, it is, so you will have to baseline to find out whether this person uses the word *never* when he is being truthful. You'll also have to look for clusters of tells. If he answered saying "I have never" he could be trying to convince, right? So I would ask the question one more time, to see whether I could get a definitive yes or no to indicate truthfulness. Keep asking the same question until you get the answer you need. Don't give up! Too many people give up right before they prove the deceptive tell or prove truthfulness.

Response #2: "I have tried my best to teach teenagers that drugs are bad."

The immediate question that comes to my mind is, *And what? Failed?* When people say, "I tried my best," that should tell you that they failed at what they tried to do. In this case, I don't care if the subject tried his best; I want to know if he sold drugs to teenagers. Ask the question again, because the subject did not answer the question. Again, we're looking for a yes or a no.

Response #3: "All I can say is I never sold drugs to teenagers."

When people use the qualifier "all I can say," they are basically telling you "I can't tell you everything," plain and simple. Why can't they tell you? Probably because it will incriminate them or someone they know. Ask the question again, because the subject did not answer it this time, either.

Response #4: "I never really talk to teenagers."

First, I don't care; second, you didn't answer the question; and third, there's that word "never" again. You already know that the word "really" is often used by liars to reinforce their lies to make them appear more truthful. It can also indicate that there is something else on the subject's mind. In this instance the subject might be saying that he never talks to teenagers, but he sells drugs to them.

Response #5: "I don't recall selling drugs to teenagers."

When Bill Clinton said, "That is not my relocation. My recollection is that I did not have sexual relations with Miss Lewinsky," there were several things going on. First, there was his failure to answer yes or no; second, he didn't use contractions; and third, he used the phrase "that is not my recollection" as a substitute for no. "I don't recall" may sound like a fancy way of saying no, but it isn't a no. It is a deflection technique. You also have to take the context of the statement into consideration. If someone asked me whether in 2000 I taught a Sgt. Moorhead, I might respond with something like, "I don't recall or remember if I taught a student by the name of Sgt. Moorhead." It's very unlikely that I'd remember a student's name from 14 years ago; I can't even remember my brothers' birthdays! But it seems hard to believe that Bill Clinton couldn't remember whether he had ever touched Monica Lewinsky's breasts in the Oval Office! Likewise, the subject in our Q&A would have remembered selling drugs to teenagers, so he still didn't answer the question. Your responsibility is to ask it again and try rephrasing it like this: "Yes or no: Did you sell drugs to teenagers?" Now there is no way this guy can get out of giving you a definitive answer; if he still refuses and spins another narrative answer, he is almost certainly being deceptive. (For an important caveat regarding the use of yes-or-no questions, please see my personal story at the end of this section, about when I was subpoenaed as a prosecution witness and forced to testify against a detainee.)

Response #6: "You know I couldn't sell to teenagers."

The use of "you know" always makes me laugh. No, I don't know: I don't know anything about you or what you did, which is why I was asking you in the first place! I would repeat the question again: "Yes or no: Did you see drugs to teenagers?"

Response #7: "Obviously I would not sell drugs to them."

The word "obviously" is similar to "you know." In this case I would ask, "Why would it be obvious that you wouldn't sell drugs? It isn't obvious to me." Then I would follow up with the question again: "Yes or no: Did you sell drugs to teenagers?" In this statement you can see that the subject also uses a non-contracted denial.

Let me share what happened to me when I was on the stand being cross-examined by the defense attorney during the military tribunal I was involved in at GTMO a few years ago. I can't share all the details of the questions asked or the information I provided, but I can share this: I was asked a yes-or-no question by the defense that I refused to answer on the stand. I answered in the narrative because it was a leading question. If I had answered yes, it would have falsely incriminated me; and if I had answered no, it would have falsely incriminated me for something else. I'm an expert in questioning techniques, so I wasn't about to be trapped with his leading question. My refusal to answer with a yes or a no infuriated the defense lawyer as well as the judge, who slammed down his gavel and demanded to know why I wouldn't answer the question properly. I told him that the question was a leading question, and I wasn't going to be trapped into a false admission. He ordered that the question be struck from the record and told the lawyer to rephrase it. He was pissed, but I stood my ground. In fact, a writer for one newspaper wrote that I "stood my ground" as I "sparred with the defense attorney." *That's right,* I thought. *Don't mess with an interrogator!* I am sharing this with you because these kinds of questions can trap people into a false confession. So be sure to properly phrase your yes-or-no questions in such a way as to eliminate any vagueness. If people feel that answering a yes-or-no question could falsely incriminate them, they simply won't answer.

Here's another mock Q&A to illustrate some verbal hot spots:

Question: "Did you answer my questions truthfully?

Response #1: "I believe so."

How about a yes or no? The word "believe" is a terribly noncommittal word. Other noncommittal words are *think*, *guess*, *suppose*, *figure*, and *assume*. Ask the question again.

Response #2: "I swear to God I am telling you the truth."

Again, where's the yes or no answer? You already know that deceptive subjects often use mild oaths to try to make their statements sound more convincing. Deceptive people are more likely than truthful people to sprinkle their statements with expressions such as "I swear," "on my honor," "as God is my witness," and "cross my heart." Truthful witnesses are more confident that the facts will prove the veracity of their statements, and thus feel less of a need to back their statements with oaths. Remember to baseline, though, because some people use this phrase all the time.

•••••

Now that you have a good handle on a variety of verbal deceptive tells, it's time to start getting to the truth. Before we jump into our questioning techniques, however (some of which you've already seen in the previous examples), you'll want to prep the person you think is lying to you, to make him feel good and thus *want* to tell you the truth. The way you do this is by inflating his pride and ego, just a bit. We want to make him feel good to create rapport. This brings us to step three, use "pride and ego up," or what Janine Driver calls "assigning positive traits."

Step 3: Use "Pride and Ego Up"

This is a technique I used as an interrogator and still use in my everyday life to make people feel good about themselves. Sometimes I'm sincere and I truly value what a person has done; and sometimes I use it to get something I want: cooperation, a positive attitude, information, or a favor. That makes me sound like an awful person, right? I don't use it to get my friends or family to do things for me! I use it to get out of speeding tickets; I use it to appease the type-A personalities at work to keep a harmonious work environment; and I use it to inspire my friends and colleagues to take chances and start their own businesses or write their own books. These things aren't bad or malicious. Well, maybe trying to get out of a speeding ticket is a bit selfish, but it's certainly not malicious. I use pride and ego up to "prime" individuals to tell me the truth. For example, if you tell a suspect that you know she is honest, has integrity, makes the right choices, cares for others, is looked up to by others and respected for doing the right thing, and so on, before going in to extract the truth, she will be more likely to tell you the truth than not. Studies show that people who take a polygraph or appear in court and "swear to tell the whole truth, nothing but the truth," tell the truth because they have been primed to—by a machine and an oath. You can ask a subject up-front, with sincerity, "Will you tell me the truth in response to what I'm about to ask you?" If she consents, she may feel that she has locked herself in to telling the truth, according to some moral code. Or you can simply state, "I want you to be truthful when I ask you these questions."

Here's how I used pride and ego up with my detainees. I would tell them, "I know you believe in your cause and I respect you for that," or "I heard that your dedication and honesty is unmatched by others you trained with," or "I know you do the right thing to protect yourself and your family, even if I don't think it's the right thing." As I said these things, I could see their pride and ego inflating right before my eyes: They would sit up straighter, roll their shoulders back, lift their chin. In short, they would began to look and feel more confident. But what it did best was that it made them feel as though they had to prove to me how dedicated, honest, and good they were—even though that meant they had to tell me incriminating information that could get them locked up for life. At the end of my interrogations I would thank them for being so honest with me, and tell them how good they should feel, knowing they had integrity. I got a lot of information using this technique. The amazing thing is that even after they "broke" and told me the truth, they would still walk out of the interrogation looking and feeling proud. Trust me, this technique works!

Every human being wants to feel proud of who they are, no matter what they have done. So before you fire off your sharpened questioning techniques, use pride and ego up first.

Step 4: Ask Good Questions

Do you think you ask good questions? Think hard about your answer, then ask yourself this again after you read what I'm about to teach you regarding the art of questioning, which is my forté. In this final step to getting to the truth, I will give you eight types of questions to use.

1. Ask a narrative question to get a narrative response.

If you are looking for narrative-type information, you must ask a narrative question. A narrative question begins with one of the six interrogatives: who, what, where, when, why, or how. Avoid asking vague narrative questions. If you want specific details, you'll need ask specific questions. For example, if you want to know what, exactly, your witness saw at the scene of the fire, you wouldn't ask, "What did you see?" Yes, it's a narrative question, but it's too vague. Your subject may respond with something like, "I saw people standing around." That tells you nothing. So in order to not waste anyone's time in getting to the pertinent information, make your narrative question more specific: "At 6:40 p.m., when you said you arrived at the scene of the fire, how many people did you see?" If you wanted find out whether he spoke to anyone who was standing around the fire, you wouldn't ask him that point blank, because it would create a space for him to be evasive. Instead, assume he spoke to others and simply ask, "What did the others say to you?" If he didn't speak to anyone, he can just say so. You've saved time by not having to ask two questions; you only had to ask one and you received the answer to both. Anyone who conducts interviews or interrogations as a normal part of their job knows that there is never enough time, and the few seconds saved by having to ask one question versus two can be crucial. So let's say you want to find out whether someone has children. Instead of asking, "Do you have children?" just assume he does and ask, "How many children do you have?" Again, if he doesn't have any, he will say so.

2. Ask yes-or-no questions, cautiously.

I've already given you many examples of these questions and how they can be used. Use them for a singular purpose: to test for truthfulness. Do not use them as a crutch or make the mistake of asking them repeatedly; this is a bad questioning technique, because if you don't ask narrative questions, you won't get information. When asking yes-or-no questions, you should try to get a yes or no response within three tries. If you don't, you will know that the subject is avoiding the question and likely hiding something.

3. Ask "Really?"

I love this one-word question and I used it frequently as an interrogator, but it does require that you have some patience. It's effective because most people are uncomfortable with silence in a conversation, so they will feel more inclined to break the silence and keep talking. Asking "Really?" encourages your subject to provide more information without your even having to ask. How cool is that? Especially when rapport and emotions are hanging in a delicate balance, you don't want to hammer someone with questions if they are still deciding whether they like or trust you enough to divulge their information. If silence makes you uncomfortable, this is when you will need patience. You can't be the one to break the silence! You asked your question, now wait for the response. If you don't, you just devalued your own question, and it will look as though you are waffling. Waiting for a response sends the message that you are in control, even if you wait in silence for three or more minutes, waiting for the subject to elaborate. This is a great technique to use if you suspect someone is lying. It also gives the subject an opportunity to amend or add to his or her statement without having to backpedal or lose too much face: "Well, maybe it didn't happen just like that" or "Now that I think about it, this is what happened."

4. Ask "How did that make you feel?"

I've mentioned that liars don't think about the feelings they should have when they lie. If you ask someone how something made him feel, he won't be able to conjure up sincere feelings for something he hasn't done, seen, experienced, or felt. At this point you'll probably hear some stuttering and stalling techniques. It is very difficult for liars to *feel* fake emotions, so when they do come up with an answer, they won't be very convincing. For example, let's say your son Sam comes home from school with bruises on his arms; he's depressed and completely withdrawn. You ask him what the problem is and finally drag it out of him that another kid at school, Patrick, is bullying him. You, your son, Patrick, and Patrick's mother all meet up in the principal's office. Patrick has repeatedly told his mother that he wasn't the one who hit Sam. He claims it was another student, Tommy. At this point it's his word against Sam's because there are no witnesses. So the mediator in this scenario, likely the principal, should ask Patrick, "How did it make you feel when Tommy bullied Sam and hit him?" If Patrick says, "I don't know," you've got him, but you still need to expose the truth. If Patrick hesitates and squirms around, obviously trying to think of how he should have felt, you've got him again, but you still have to expose the truth. If Patrick says, "It made me feel bad," the principle needs to come back and ask, "Really?" And dive deeper: "Why did it make you feel bad, Patrick?" or "Why didn't you stop Tommy?" Let Patrick incriminate himself before you accuse him, because Patrick's mother will shut you down in a heartbeat if you accuse her son of bullying. Keep asking non-accusatory, narrative questions until you break Patrick's will to resist telling the truth.

5. Ask follow-up questions to fully exploit information.

Listen carefully and analyze every word people say when answering your questions. Follow up on all topics they tell you to extract all of the details. Remember this saying: Exploit all verbs and define all nouns. If I tell you I am going the movies tonight, you have to fully exploit "going" and define "movies" and "tonight." How am I going? By car, by foot, by train? How long will it take me to get there? Who am I going with? When am I going? Why am I going? What movie am I going to see? Where are the movies located? Ask "What else?" "What other?" "Who else?" "Where else?" "When else?" and "How else?" to exploit the information you have and get all of the details. For example, let's say you ask me, "Who are you going with?" and I reply, "Alissa." Am I only going with Alissa? Maybe I'm going with someone else. To find out you must ask a follow-up question: "Who else are you going with?" Keep going until you hear me say, "I'm not going with anyone else." Now you have fully exploited who I'm going with. Truthful people may just come right out and say, "I'm going with Alissa, Diane, and Kristy." But deceptive people will make you work for the entire answer, just as my detainees did. We have two ears and one mouth, so it makes sense that we should listen twice as much as we speak. In the interrogation world, we listen intently more than we speak because we are listening to the details, and listening for verbal deceptive tells, so we can ask follow-up questions.

6. Ask the same question twice.

This is a simple questioning technique that is commonly used to check for truthfulness and accuracy of information provided. Let's say you ask your subject, "When did you first notice the gun was missing," and your subject answers, "When I checked the safe this morning." Let 10 or 15 minutes go by and ask the same exact question again to see if your suspect responds with the same answer. If he answers, "When I checked the safe last night," you know you have a discrepancy that you need to exploit. Use the timeline method and your questioning techniques to fully exploit the discrepancy. Your suspect may have legitimately made a mistake and explain it was for certain this morning; or he may have lied and forgot the details of his lie. Don't be accusatory; use the techniques in this book before you lose rapport and shut him down.

7. Ask a control question.

Control questions are a bit more complicated than repeat questions, but they are a great tool to check for truthfulness and accuracy. I'll use the same example from the previous page. After your suspect tells you, "When I checked the safe this morning," instead of asking the same question again to see if he gives the same answer, change up the information a bit when you rephrase the question. So instead, maybe ask, "The first time you noticed the gun missing was when you checked the safe last night, right?" This is a yes-or-no question, but if the suspect is being truthful, he should pick up on the fact you changed his answer and correct you. If he fails to spot the inconsistency, does that mean he was lying? Or was he just not paying attention to what you asked? You'll have to find out.

8. Ask non-pertinent questions.

You might be wondering why you would ever need to get irrelevant information. Isn't the whole purpose of this book to teach you how to extract truthful *pertinent* information? Yes, but the other purpose, which I mentioned way back in the Introduction, is how to extract information while maintaining rapport. This technique is how you do just that. When you start to see the body language shift in your subject, especially if she is closing off to you physically, you need to bring her back to a more relaxed frame of mind by letting up on the stress and tension. A way to do this is by asking a non-pertinent question. Ask her about topics that make her feel comfortable. Even if you are on the brink of getting a confession, you won't get it if your subject shuts down. Trust me, as I'm speaking from experience. Take the time to relax your subject so she can regain her composure. Confessions come when people are relaxed and feeling trusting. You may want to ask her about her family, her favorite sport or hobby, or what she likes to watch on TV or listen to on the radio. Get her comfortable and talking again. After she is feeling more relaxed you can go back to your pertinent questions, but do so delicately. A conversation often brings about an ebb and flow of emotions, so you will have to go with the flow.

You now have eight really solid questioning techniques to catch lies. Now you need to know the three types of questions to avoid because they will only frustrate you and the person you are questioning, and hinder you from obtaining detailed, specific information.

Questions to Always Avoid Asking

Don't ask leading questions.

Leading questions are questions that are phrased in a way to get the answer you want, not necessarily the true answer. Lawyers use this technique all the time because it works. When I was on the stand during the military tribunal, the defense lawyer asked me a leading question: "Isn't it true that in my client's culture, the perception of females is different than an American's perception?" I said yes, and as soon as that word came out of my mouth, I wanted to suck it back in. He got me. He led me into saying yes so that it would appear to the courtroom that I knew I made my detainee uncomfortable, which was not the case. The lawyer did a little happy dance and said, "No further questions, Your Honor." I was so angry at myself, which is probably why I sparred with him the next time he asked me a leading question, and every time after that! Getting the information you think you want to hear is not necessarily truthful information. If you are not a lawyer, don't use leading questions. If you are ever on the stand, don't fall victim to them. Refuse to answer yes or no and state why: it's a leading question, and the lawyer is leading you to what she wants to hear. (Sorry, lawyers—your secret's out!)

Don't ask compound questions.

Ask one question at a time, always! If you ask two questions at once, you will miss important information. Deceptive people love to be asked compound questions, because if someone doesn't want to give up information, this is the perfect way to avoid answering. For example, let's say you asked your employee, "Sheryl, why is the drawer coming up $100 short? Did anyone else work the register today?" If Sheryl took that $100 from the drawer, she is going to answer only one of those questions with the hope that you forget to come back and ask the other one again. Save yourself the trouble and never, ever ask a compound question; it's the perfect way for someone to get away with a lie. It also will make you look bad as an interviewer, interrogator, or questioner. You don't want to allow the suspect to control the interview. Refer back to the transcript of Larry King's interview with the Ramseys: he asks several compound questions and gets the answer to one.

Don't ask vague questions.

I've already covered this, so I am going to leave you with a saying: "If you ask a vague question, you will get a vague answer."

Ajmal (named changed for security reasons), a Pakistani detainee with whom I had built great rapport and who actually invited me to Pakistan to meet his family one day, had information on the location of a secret underground Taliban training camp in Afghanistan. He didn't want to tell me who was in charge of the camp. He went into details about where it was located and even identified its location on maps that I brought in. He told me that he would tell me anything I wanted to know except who was in charge. *Oh, a challenge!* I agreed and told him I appreciated all the information he was giving me, so I could live without knowing this one thing, while I grinned to myself, thinking, *You'll tell me by the time I'm done and you won't even realize it when you do.* Ajmal loved to smoke cigarettes, so I offered him a cigarette break in every interrogation session, which he appreciated. My interpreter and I would step out of the interrogation booth to take a break since I hated the smoke. My plan was to trick to Ajmal into telling me who ran the camp solely by skillfully controlling the conversation and inserting the right question at the right time. It was a simple plan, but it wasn't easy. Ajmal had to be relaxed enough in order to let his guard down and forget he didn't want to tell me that piece of information. That meant I had to downplay the importance of it by not talking about it, and, if it came up, by not showing facial expressions leaked happiness, contempt, or surprise. I briefed my interpreter about my plan to trick Ajmal into telling me who ran the camp. He agreed and was eager to play along. Ajmal finished the cigarette, and we went back inside and continued the interrogation. After three hours of dancing around the subject and getting Ajmal laughing and completely relaxed, I inserted a control question. I simply said, "When Abdullah ran the camp, how many fighters could he train at one time?" Ajmal replied, "Abdullah didn't run the camp; Abdul Rahman did, but anywhere from 50 to 200 fighters would be there." Then there was silence. All three of us looked at each other; my interpreter and I had a grin on our faces (we couldn't help it—our plan had worked after all this time!), while Ajmal looked puzzled. He suddenly grabbed his mouth in shock as his eyes flew open. He realized that he had been caught. I told him that I didn't want to trick him but that I really needed that one piece of information. Knowing when to insert the perfectly phrased question is the key to successful truth extraction. I was able to extract that name without Ajmal's buzzer going off. It took me three hours to do it, and I was mentally exhausted at the end, but it was worth every minute.

Congratulations! You have just completed my five-step program to detecting deception and getting to the truth. Now get out there and use it!

11

Your Toolkit for Reading Body Language

This chapter is your quick and handy reference guide to my five-step body language and deception-detecting program. Practice it and use it!

You Are Not a Mind Reader

Prepare yourself for success, and don't fall victim to the myths about body language.

- Remember to **use my rule of three** for detecting deceptive tells: baseline, look for clusters, and be aware of context.

- **Overcome inattentional blindness.** We don't see what we don't expect to see; so before you begin to read body language, whether is it to build rapport, mirror personality traits, or detect deception, you must rid yourself of all biases, prejudices, or assumptions. If you assume anything, you will unconsciously turn your assumptions into a false reality.

- How many times have you lost something and you can't find it for days because you keep looking for it where you assumed it would be? Or how many times has your tempered flared with your significant other because you were assuming he or she was up to no good? Gather the facts and evidence first, without the assumptions; assumptions will mislead you and blind you to the truth. Also, try to be more trusting of others; if you automatically don't trust anyone, you will see deceptive behavior everywhere, even in truthful people.

Lying 101

Three types of lies: false statement, embellishment, and lies by omission.

Two types of liars: imploders (everyday liars) and exploders (powerful liars).

The four secrets to being a good liar:

1. Remain confident.
2. The devil is in the details: details are the death of a lie.
3. Plan and prepare.
4. Exhibit congruence in your body language.

My Five-Step Process for Reading Body Language: Be a Body-Language Expert; Be a REBLE

1. R is for relax

Remember: If you feel stupid, you look stupid. Confidence doesn't come from knowing everything and always being right; it comes from learning from our mistakes when we are wrong.

- Take a power pose and a belly breath. Here are your power poses for looking and feeling confident:
  - Stand like Superman or Wonder Woman.
  - Steeple (basketball, low, high, and handgun).
  - Sit in the José pose.
  - Assume the gorilla pose.
  - Use Hitler hands (as a last resort only).
  - Show your thumbs of power.

- Never hide your hands.
- Do a hand- or headstand.

2. E is for establish rapport

10 rapport-building techniques:

1. Smile.
2. Use touch, carefully.
3. Share something about yourself (*quid pro quo*).
4. Mirror and match, cautiously.
5. Respect others.
6. Use open body language.
7. Suspend your ego .
8. Flatter and praise.
9. Take your time and listen.
10. Get the person talking and moving.

Five tips for enhanced communication skills:

1. Manage your emotions; sometimes we are speaking to the role not the person, so don't take it personally.
2. Agree to disagree.
3. Be aware.
4. Favorably influence people.
5. Don't be afraid to let them teach you.

Personality preferences: Talk and act like others to make them feel more comfortable. Mirror and match personality preferences.

- **The Extravert vs. the Introvert** dichotomy tells us how we prefer to get energized. Extraverts get energized by being around activity and other people; Introverts get energized by being by themselves or with a few close friends in a quiet environment.

- **The INtuitive vs. the Sensor** dichotomy is how we prefer to take in information. INtuitives like to take on a task by conceptualizing and seeing the big-picture outcome first; then they break down the processes and tasks they need to get there. Sensors prefer to create rules and processes first, which take them to the concept of the project they have been assigned.

- **The Thinker vs. the Feeler** dichotomy tells us how we prefer to make decisions. If you know you are making a decision as a Thinker and the outcome may upset others, you will have to make sure you use a few rapport techniques when informing those affected by your decision so you are not perceived as indifferent, insensitive, or unfeeling.

- **The Judger vs. the Perceiver** dichotomy is all about how we prefer to organize the world around us. Judgers like to get things done on schedule and like closure. They work best with deadlines and guidelines. Unlike Judgers, Perceivers will wait until the last minute to make a decision; they like to keep their options open. They are open to ideas and changes and because of this, they are more flexible than the more rigid Judgers.

3. B is for baseline

Baseline people by talking to them for a few minutes to see how they normally act and sound. Make sure you baseline while they are relaxed and calm. Then ask pertinent questions or switch to an important topic and watch for deviations in their baseline behavior. Make sure to look for clusters of tells (at least three) and understand the context in which the information is being delivered (that is, is the person sick, scared, in shock, on medications, suffering from a physical or mental aliment, and so on).

4. L is for look for deviations

Observing the body for behavioral incongruence:

1. **Human emotions and facial leakage:** The seven basic human emotions are: anger, fear, disgust, surprise, happiness, sadness, and contempt. Look for micro-expressions (facial leakage) such as duping delight.

2. **The head:** Look for behavioral incongruence when a person says yes or no. Does the body match up with the words?

3. **Lying eyes:**

   - Eye contact: Some liars will give you a hard stare; others will look shifty and break eye contact. Both can be indicators of deception.

   - Rapid eye blinking is a physiological response to the body drying out from stress and anxiety.

   - A prolonged eye blink can indicate a strong emotion, concentration, and/or deception.

   - Use NLP and Grinder and Bandler's eye accessing cue chart:

     – Looking up is accessing the visual sense, either to recall information (up and to the left) or create/construct information (up and to the right).

     – Looking at about ear level is accessing the auditory sense to recall information (to the left) or create/construct information (up and to the right).

     – Looking down and to the left is accessing the kinesthetic senses, feelings both recalled and constructed; down and to the right is engaging in an internal dialogue.

   - With NLP you must look for patterns in eye movements and establish a baseline before you can use it as a tool to detect deception. To baseline someone quickly, ask, "What is the fifth word in the 'Star Spangled Banner'?"

4. **The mouth:** Swallowing hard is a physiological response to the body drying out from stress and anxiety. The lips get thin and even disappear when people are uncomfortable and angry.

5. **The hands:**

   - Hiding hands hides the emotions.
   - Closed palms can indicate untrustworthiness, or the fact that someone is keeping something, an emotion or a thought, to him- or herself.
   - Hand to head (face, neck, top of head) usually indicates high stress and untrustworthiness.
   - Hand to mouth can indicate disapproval, deep thought, an internal dialogue, or deception.
   - Hand to chin can indicate power, boredom, or contemplation.
   - Hand to neck can indicate tension in the muscles— "you are a pain in my neck"—or deception.
   - Head scratching can indicate deep thought, confusion, or disbelief.

6. **The six signs of uncertainty:**

   1. Shoulder shrug.
   2. Balling up.
   3. The fig leaf.
   4. Self-preening (using self-pacifiers).
   5. Stepping back.
   6. The body shift.

7. **The Pinocchio effect:** An itchy nose can be a sign of deception.

5. E is for extract the truth

The four steps for extracting the truth:

Step 1: Timeline events: Use the timelining technique to gather all details and break apart a cover story.

Step 2: Look for verbal hot spots/deceptive tells:

1. Pronoun usage for distancing (no "I" or "my").
2. Verb tense changes.
3. Non-contracted denials ("I did not have sexual relations with that woman...").
4. Cannot say yes or no/dodges the question.
5. *Never* is not *no*.
6. Stalling techniques: answering a question with a question, repeating a question back, using filler words.
7. Hedging statements, such as the "but syndrome," the oath hedge, and "actually."
8. Distancing language.
9. Softening language.
10. Text bridges.

Step 3: Use "pride and ego up": Tell people how honest and truthful they are so they will be honest and truthful with you.

Step 4: Ask good questions:

1. Ask a narrative question to get a narrative response.
2. Ask yes-or-no questions, cautiously.
3. Ask "Really?"
4. Ask "How did that make you feel?"
5. Ask follow-up questions to fully exploit information.
6. Ask a repeat question.
7. Ask a control question.
8. Ask non-pertinent questions.

Three questions to avoid:

1. Leading questions.
2. Compound questions.
3. Vague questions.

Afterword

Have you ever been a victim of a scam? An incident just happened to me and I want to share it with you for two reasons. First, it's a great example of why I wrote this book; and second, if you happen to receive the same phone call I did, it's my hope that you can protect yourself from this IRS phishing scam.

One day there was a strange automated phone message on my phone saying, "We have been trying to contact you. Please contact the IRS in regards to a claim filed against you. Please call 202-657-5115 (yes, that was the number!) for your case number." Initially I started to panic but then I became angry because I have always been a good citizen and paid my taxes. I even get a refund most years because I pay so much up-front! Anyway, I called the number and a male with a foreign accent answered, "IRS?" He collected my name and address and then told me there was a discrepancy in my taxes from the years 2008 to 2012. He claimed I'd been sent numerous notifications and because I hadn't responded to them, an officer was coming to arrest me and put a lien against all of my assets. My bank account would even be frozen. I knew immediately that something was very wrong. I fired back with, "My father is CPA and I get *paid* every year by the IRS! Provide me in writing the dates of all notifications that were sent to me and where they were sent, because I never received any!" *How dare they threaten me?* I thought. As the guy started launching into his threats again, which sounded as though they were being read from a script in front of him, I began to doubt everything he was saying. I have to admit, I went a bit "Rhode Island" on him. (If you have never angered an Italian from Rhode Island, consider yourself lucky, because when we get angry, we tend to off go off like a Roman candle.) The guy on the other end of the line had no idea who he was dealing with. He said, "Ma'am, you need to calm down, because you can't talk to an IRS officer this way."

"Oh yes I can," I fired back. "And again, I demand proof of these so-called notifications. Tell me the date the first one was sent and where it was sent to." He started reading from his script again, but I cut him off: "Stop reading your script and answer my question! Where and when were these notifications sent?"

He started to get flustered and fumbled his words. Then after a long silence he said he was going to get his supervisor, and I was put on interminable hold. His "supervisor" got on the phone, another male with a foreign accent, and said, "Ma'am, the notifications were sent to your billing address."

"Okay, and what address would that be?" Silence. That's what I thought.

I hung up the phone and called my dad. He wasn't home, but my mom answered and I told her what had just happened. She said, "Oh, no way! It's a scam." She looked up the number and it was cell phone that traced back to Maryland. I told her I'd call her right back. I called the "IRS" again. The same man answered, but this time, instead of saying "IRS" as he picked up, he said (sounding very professional), "This is Officer So-and-So with the Internal Revenue Service." I laughed to myself.

"Hi, it's me again," I said with a smile, "Please give me the spelling of your first and last name so I can give my CPA your name and number so he can call you about this discrepancy." More silence. I said, "That's what I thought. I just want you to know that I have reported you to the authorities and to the IRS phishing fraud hotline."

On the other end I heard, "Wh-What? Uh—"

I cut him off and said, "Your little scam stops with me," and hung up.

I did indeed report them to the IRS and I hope they can track these criminals down. They took 20 minutes of my life and made my blood pressure rise. No one should have to go through something like this, and I hope no one has fallen victim to their scam and given these crooks money.

Rest assured that you won't fall victim to any scam if you use my program. Now that you've read this book, you know how to relax and gain the confidence to stand up for yourself (you don't have to go Rhode Island on anyone), you know how to establish rapport, you know what to listen and look for in order to baseline behavior, you know how to look for deviations from the baseline and deceptive tells, and, finally, you know how to use the art of questioning to get to the truth. I definitely stood up to these creeps, even though my rapport was, well, kind of non-existent because I didn't care about them liking me. The guy's baseline was that he read a script and had no answers outside of what was provided there. His deviations included an inability to answer my questions, stalling, fumbling for words, putting me on hold for a very long time, and getting flustered when I started to get irate, which was complete change from the calm, authoritative voice he used when he told me that I was going to be arrested and my assets would be frozen. And finally, when I asked him to provide proof of the previous notifications, he couldn't. Of course the clincher was his reluctance to give me his name. Oh, and they had no idea what a CPA was—seriously?

I usually do things for a purpose. I have conversations with a purpose (to extract information), I use specific words for a purpose (to mirror/match and establish common ground with someone), and I use body language with a purpose (to build rapport and to look and feel confident). I even chose the number of chapters in this book (11) for a reason. I purposely choose this number because it is an important one in my life. The number 11 appears in part of my company's logo, the congruent symbol for The Congruency Group, as it is said to represent intuition and awareness, as well as wisdom that's not yet being tapped into. (This number was also integral to my experience at GTMO, but unfortunately I cannot share why.)

In the 11 chapters you just read, hopefully you have learned techniques to help you tap into your inner confidence, build rapport, enhance your interpersonal communications, win people over, earn trust and respect, interpret your gut feelings, read body language, detect deception verbally and nonverbally, get to the truth, and, really, anything else that will empower you in your personal and professional life.

I truly hope you have enjoyed this book as much as I enjoyed writing it. I wish you success in all of your endeavors. Hopefully the new tools I have offered you will help you achieve all your goals and aspirations. I know they can; I've used them myself and wrote this book for you.

With sincerest gratitude,

Lena Sisco

Index

About the Author

Lena Sisco is a former Department of Defense (DoD) interrogator and has used her interrogation and deception-detecting techniques on members of al Qaeda and the Taliban during the Global War on Terror while she was stationed in Guantanamo Bay, Cuba, in 2002.

Lena has a master's in archaeology and art from Brown University, and has excavated overseas as an archaeologist. She is a former Navy Intelligence officer who has been training the DoD since 2003 in detecting deception, behavioral congruency, elicitation, interrogation methods, tactical questioning, strategic interviewing, cross-cultural communications, enemy prisoner of war psychology, working with interpreters, and site exploitation.

She is president and cofounder of The Congruency Group and a senior instructor at the Body Language Institute in Washington, D.C. Her company's motto is "Move your body to influence your mind; read the body to influence people." Aside from training individuals and organizations on how to detect deception and get to the truth, through advanced interviewing techniques, Lena also teaches the science of body language as well as the skill of enhanced communications and the art of rapport-building. Her goal is to help people enhance their interpersonal skills and gain that leading edge in both their personal and professional lives.

A popular keynote speaker, Lena has also appeared on the Dr. Drew Headline News Network as a body-language expert, and was featured in *Twist* as a body-language expert. She has trained small-business owners, arson investigators, auditors, pediatric dentists, and member of the Special Forces.

Lena is originally from Rhode Island and looks forward to getting back there soon to help manage the horse farm her parents just bought. She is an animal lover who has volunteered her time as a zookeeper aide and animal caretaker at AZA accredited organizations. She believes she has lived two lives: the first, as an archaeologist (her childhood dream); and the second, as an interrogator. She hopes in her third life she will be training animals. Until then, she'll keep busy with her other passions: writing and teaching.